PENGUIN

IT'S A CITY-SHOWMAN'S SHOW!

DR IMRE BANGHA is Lecturer in Hindi at the University of Oxford and Head of the Alexander Csoma de Körös Centre for Oriental Studies at Sapientia—the Hungarian University of Transylvania, Romania. He studied Indology in Budapest and holds a PhD in Hindi from Visva-Bharati. His publications include English, Hindi and Hungarian books and articles on Brajbhāṣā and other forms of early Hindi, with special focus on the poetic works of Ānandghan, Ṭhākur, Viṣṇudās, Tulsīdās, Bājīd as well as on Rekhta literature.

R.C.C. FYNES was educated at the University of Leeds and the Queen's College, Oxford. His previous publications include English translations of the Sanskrit texts of Hemacandra's *The Lives of the Jain Elders* and Jinaratna's *The Epitome of Queen Lilavati*.

He is currently a Principal Lecturer in the Faculty of Art, Design and Humanities, De Montfort University, Leicester.

IT'S A CITY-SHOWMAN'S SHOW!

Transcendental Songs of Ānandghan

Translated with an introduction by
Imre Bangha and R.C.C. Fynes

Foreword by
John E. Cort

PENGUIN BOOKS

PENGUIN BOOKS
Published by the Penguin Group
Penguin Books India Pvt. Ltd, 11 Community Centre, Panchsheel Park, New Delhi 110 017, India
Penguin Group (USA) Inc., 375 Hudson Street, New York, New York 10014, USA
Penguin Group (Canada), 90 Eglinton Avenue East, Suite 700, Toronto, Ontario, M4P 2Y3, Canada (a division of Pearson Penguin Canada Inc.)
Penguin Books Ltd, 80 Strand, London WC2R 0RL, England
Penguin Ireland, 25 St Stephen's Green, Dublin 2, Ireland (a division of Penguin Books Ltd)
Penguin Group (Australia), 707 Collins Street, Melbourne, Victoria 3008, Australia (a division of Pearson Australia Group Pty Ltd)
Penguin Group (NZ), 67 Apollo Drive, Rosedale, Auckland 0632, New Zealand (a division of Pearson New Zealand Ltd)
Penguin Books (South Africa) (Pty) Ltd, Block D, Rosebank Office Park, 181 Jan Smuts Avenue, Parktown North, Johannesburg 2193, South Africa

Penguin Books Ltd, Registered Offices: 80 Strand, London WC2R 0RL, England

First published by Penguin Books India 2013

10 9 8 7 6 5 4 3 2 1

ISBN 9780143415558

[redacted]

Typeset in Bembo by Eleven Arts, Delhi
Printed at HT Media Limited, Noida

Contents

Acknowledgements

As the proper beginning to any traditional Indian work is the *guruvandanā*—the giving of respect and acknowledgement for the guidance without which it would not have reached fruition—it is our pleasant task to begin this work with our expression of gratitude to the people who have freely guided us with their advice throughout the writing of this book.

Our deepest gratitude is to the two learned teachers of early Hindi, Professor Govind Sharma in Vrindaban and Dr Kishorilal in Naini, near Allahabad, who selflessly offered us their time and expertise in interpreting early modern texts. They have transmitted a knowledge accumulated over centuries, a learning now largely neglected. It is a great loss for students of Indian literature that both of them passed away before the publication of this book.

In addition to writing the Foreword to this book, Professor John E. Cort of Denison University, Granville, Ohio, gave continuous encouragement and we have profited from his learned comments on our manuscript. Professor Kumarpal Desai in Ahmedabad offered his invaluable inputs on Ānandghan and Shri Jagdishdas Rathaur gave some important comments from the standpoint of his expertise in Rajasthani. We are also grateful to Dr Paul Dundas from the University of Edinburgh for his help in specifying some Jain technical terms and to Dr Katherine Butler Brown of King's College, London, whose advice helped us to a better understanding of the musical aspect of Ānandghan's songs. Professor Denis Matringe of the CNRS, Paris, offered his transliteration and translation of a song by Bulhe Shah to enable comparison with a similar one by Ānandghan. The book also benefited from the excellent technical skills of Dr Csaba Dezső from Eötvös Loránd University, Budapest.

Dr Daksha Mistry from M.S. University, Vadodara provided us with photocopies of manuscripts collected on her extensive research trips to Rajasthan. Two important handwritten books from Bikaner were also copied for our project by Dr Francesca Orsini, SOAS, London, in 2007. Access to manuscripts and published material was granted at the Jaipur, Jodhpur and Bikaner branches of the Rajasthan Oriental Research Institute, at Acharya Shri Vinayanand Jnan Bhandar, Jaipur; the Abhay Jain Granthalay, Bikaner; Rajasthani Research Institute, Chopasni; Hindi Sahitya Sammelan, Allahabad; and at the Oriental Institute, Vadodara. We are grateful to the directors and staff of these institutions.

Our idea of translating Ānandghan together was born at De Montfort University in Leicester, in the vicinity of the Jain Centre. The early encouragement of Professor Harunaga Isaacson and Dr Dominic Goodall was a vital stimulus for the project.

The Max Mueller Memorial Fund and the Sub-Faculty of South and Inner Asian Studies at the University of Oxford provided funding for two study tours in India in 2006 and 2007, where among other matters the poems of Ānandghan were discussed with local experts and manuscripts were copied and consulted.

Foreword

An important development in Jain studies over the past several decades has been for scholars to see the myriad ways in which Jains have participated in all aspects of South Asian religion and culture for more than two millennia. That participation has often been marked by a distinctly Jain content and style, and so one needs to be versed in the rich and distinctively Jain world of cosmology, soteriology, metaphysics, ritual, literature and social forms to gain a fuller understanding of the Jain expressions of the shared Indic religious culture. At the same time, however, Jains have not been in a bounded and sealed cultural ghetto. Jains have actively engaged with all manner of non-Jains, and so any attempt to adequately understand South Asian religion and culture is impoverished to the extent that it ignores the Jains. The work of Imre Bangha and Richard Fynes on the seventeenth-century poet and hymnist Ānandghan—an important figure who has hitherto received scant attention in European-language scholarship—shows that this observation applies as well to the study of north Indian vernacular religious literature of the past half-millennium.

This literature is generally situated within a framework broadly characterized as *bhakti* or devotion. Bhakti as a mode of religiosity emerged gradually in South Asia more than two thousand years ago. I have shown elsewhere that the Jains have been significant participants in the practice of bhakti since its earliest developments (Cort 2002a). Jains have sung and recited of their relationships to God—which in their case is the Jina—in Sanskrit, Prakrit, Apabhramsa, Persian, Tamil, Kannada and the medieval and modern forms of the regional languages in every part of India where they have lived. There are, I would estimate, more manuscripts of devotional texts than of any other genre among the hundreds of thousands of manuscripts preserved by the Jains in their famous libraries. Among the vernacular languages in which Jains have composed devotional texts are Braj, Hindi and Gujarati—the same that inform the distinctive language of Ānandghan, which might simply and most accurately be termed *bhāṣā* or *bolī*, the spoken tongue. Ānandghan presents us with something of a mystery. We have his poems, a selection of which has been wonderfully brought over into English in this volume. But beyond that we know little about him. There is nothing available that is historically reliable enough to term a biography. Even when we turn to hagiography and oral tradition we are left in the end with only a glimmer of this Jain monk who seems to have just turned away, out of our sight, down a distant, solitary road.

Part of the problem of placing him is that he doesn't fit well into our models of late-medieval Śvetāmbar Mūrtipūjak Jain mendicancy. Most monks at this time were domesticated *yatis*, who observed the mendicant vows in only partial form, and served as residential priests in each local Mūrtipūjak community in western and northern India. There was only a handful of monks who maintained the five vows and other mendicant rules to the fullest, and so were known as *saṁvegī sādhus*, or seeker monks. The leader of this group during the time Ānandghan lived was Satyavijaygaṇi (1624–1700), about whom also we know little, and the intellectual inspiration of the group was Mahopādhyāy Yaśovijay (1626–88), one of the greatest intellectuals in South Asian history. But Ānandghan doesn't fit easily into either camp. A reading of his poems might suggest that he represented a third mode of mendicant conduct, one that was anti-institutional—but without being completely a Jain equivalent of antinomian—centering on freelance asceticism, meditation, and in his case, of course, on composition of poems. Such monks undoubtedly have always existed at the margins of Jain society, but due to the very nature of their lives and practices they have left little historical evidence. These spiritual outriders were viewed with suspicion by the landed yatis, whose own conduct so clearly did not match the well-articulated rules for proper Jain monks, and were threatened by expressions of true asceticism and renunciation. These free spirits have also been looked upon with suspicion by the orthoprax saṁvegī sādhus, who have emphasized the necessity of travelling in groups, in being open to the public scrutiny of both their mendicant colleagues and the more numerous Jain laity, and who have therefore in their own ways led lives of highly institutionalized asceticism and renunciation.

We can better understand Ānandghan if we place him within several other frameworks about which we know more. Ānandghan's poems give copious evidence of his familiarity with the broader universe of vernacular religious poetry of his time. Bangha and Fynes note that Ānandghan's poems in some cases have been attributed to non-Jain poets such as Kabīr, and no doubt if one searched the entirety of the ocean of late medieval poems in the vernaculars of north India one would find that a number of poems, lines and phrases are shared by Ānandghan with many other poets. This was not a time when the concepts of 'intellectual property rights' or 'plagiarism' were operational.

His poems—especially those in the *Bahattarī*, the collection from which Bangha and Fynes have made most of their selection—share the emphasis on direct experience of an inner reality with many of the poems of *nirguṇ bhakti*. Others—especially many of those in his other major collection, the *Caubīsī*—share much with the vernacular poetry that lovingly describes the tangible and visible nature of the divine, and which modern scholars have characterized as *saguṇ bhakti*. Neither of these genres is distinctly and solely 'Hindu'; both are shared by Hindus, Buddhists, Jains, Muslims, as well as others who defy any neat religious identity. Given the overlap—one is tempted even to define it as a deep intertextuality—between the poems of Ānandghan and many other poets, it is probably safe to assume that he spent as much time in the company of an array of religious seekers and poets from multiple religious and social backgrounds as he did in more orthodox and institutional Jain settings.

Ānandghan doubtless was not the only Mūrtipūjak monk to participate in these inter-denominational (and non-denominational) circles. But here we find another way in which Ānandghan poses us a historical puzzle. In the Digambar tradition of north India there is a rich, highly populated community of vernacular poets who wrote in ways that give evidence of extensive social and literary interaction with their non-Jain contemporaries. The best-known of these is the layman Banārsīdās (1586–1643), who was born in a Mūrtipūjak family but drifted out of the Mūrtipūjak fold, and spent much more time in several circles of largely Digambar poets, intellectuals and spiritual seekers. While Banārsīdās was not the first one to write Digambar bhakti poetry in Braj, he is looked upon as the most significant person in the early development of this literary tradition. In the subsequent two-and-a-half centuries there were several hundred Digambar vernacular poets in this lineage, almost all of them laymen. The verses of poets such as Dyānatrāy, Bhūdardās, Daulatrām, Bhagcandra and Budhjan, who lived in the eighteenth and nineteenth centuries, are still sung by many Digambar Jains today, and contemporary north Indian Digambar composition of *bhajans* and *pads*, devotional songs, takes place in the shadow of their influence. We have here a well-defined, extensive tradition that lasted for several centuries.

When we turn to the Mūrtipūjak communities of the past several centuries and look for the successors of Ānandghan, we find a very different situation. The extant literature about Ānandghan has references to neither an initiating guru nor a lineage of poet-monks whose works shaped his literary activities. Nor do we know of any successors to him, either in a direct guru–disciple relationship, or in terms of literary influence. He seemingly emerges from nowhere and leaves no trace other than his own poems.

However, a publication project starting in the nineteenth century—the early years of the extensive publication of Śvetāmbar texts, a project that has thrived for over a century largely independent of any external Indological, colonial or global influences—indicates one perception of a larger universe of Jain vernacular authors in which Ānandghan belonged. In the last quarter of the nineteenth century a Mūrtipūjak layman in Bombay named Bhimsingh Manak Sha published several collections of Jain texts in Sanskrit, Prakrit and some vernaculars. Among these was a series of four large collections called *Prakaraṇ Ratnākar* (Textbook Treasuries). He published these, according to the title page of the first volume, for a singular purpose: the increase of knowledge (*jñānvṛddhyarth*), a laudable and meritorious Jain field in which to strew one's wealth in donation. He published the first volume in the series in Bombay in 1876, and republished it in 1903.[1] This volume included the text of Ānandghan's *Caubīsī*, along with the prose explanatory gloss (*bālāvabodh*) by Jñānsār. The other texts that Bhimsingh Manak Sha chose to include in that thick volume of 576 pages indicate not a lineage, but rather a virtual community of like-minded Jain poets within which the editor, and presumably many others, perceived Ānandghan to belong. These include seven Gujarati texts by Yaśovijay, two by Devcandra, two Sanskrit hymns to Cintāmaṇi Pārśvanāth (the highly popular wish-granting form of the twenty-third Jina), one of which was by a layman named Malūkcand Vīrcand, and Banārsīdās's famous Braj version of the *Samayasāra* of Kundakunda, the foundational philosopher of Digambar spiritualism or mysticism (*adhyātma*).[2] The texts themselves represent a range of genres, not all of which align clearly with Ānandghan's spiritual focus. Those of Yaśovijay, for example, include an analysis of the contemporary status of Mūrtipūjak society, a study of a Yoga text by the seventh–eighth-century Haribhadra, evocations of liberation (*samādhi*) and equanimity (*samatā*), and a refutation of his Digambar contemporaries.[3]

[1] The copy of the 1903 version that I have consulted is in the collection of Harvard University's Widener Library. In some publications the editor is also called Shravak Bhimsi Manek.

[2] The copy at Harvard only contains twelve texts, and not that of Banārsīdās. But the table of contents lists Banārsīdās's *Samayasāra*, and indicates it should be found on pages 577–787. Nor do the contents of the 1903 version fully correspond to those of the 1876 volume as reported in Vinayvijay 1914:117–27, who listed fourteen texts. I cannot account for these discrepancies; but they do not materially affect my point about the community of authors and texts within which this editor located Ānandghan. The connections and overlaps in terms of content and spiritual emphasis among Ānandghan, Yaśovijay and Devcandra have more recently been explored by Shah (1993).

[3] A full study of Yaśovijay's many compositions is one of the most crucial desiderata of Jain studies. His many vernacular writings in particular have been almost totally ignored by scholars of Jainism outside of India.

Devcandra is the one other late-medieval Mūrtipūjak author who is well-known for his writings on spiritual, mystical matters similar to those on which Ānandghan focused.[4] He was a Khartar Gaccha monk who lived from 1690 until 1756. Although he was born in Bikaner, he spent most of his mendicant career in Ahmedabad. The Khartar Gaccha scholar Mahopadhyay Vinaysagar (2004:306) has adjudged Devcandra's *Caubīsī* as the only devotional text in the modern vernacular devoted to the twenty-four Jinas that is the equal of Ānandghan's. Devcandra was also the author of a number of spiritual-mystical poems. But he differed from Ānandghan in that he was deeply embedded in the institutional structures of the Khartar Gaccha, in contrast to Ānandghan's more independent stance. In addition to his hymns urging his readers and listeners to focus on the spiritual realities of their own souls, a reality that ultimately has nothing to do with the material world and even the body, Devcandra composed a number of exoteric ritual texts, including the standard liturgy for the lustration of the Jina that is performed on a regular basis in Khartar Gaccha temples throughout India today (Babb 1996:64–101). The two texts included in the *Prakaraṇ Ratnākar*, for example, are both vernacular expositions on basic matters of doctrine.[5] In this he was similar to Yaśovijay, who composed a large number of ritual liturgies, philosophical discourses and other texts of an exoteric nature. In their production of texts that have remained central to the ritual cultures of the Khartar and Tapā Gacchas, both Devcandra and Yaśovijay exhibited a breadth of literary and institutional commitments that make them stand apart from Ānandghan.

[4] Information on Devcandra comes from Desai 2003, Lalitprabhsagar 1994 and Vinaysagar 2004:305–08.

[5] They are his *Āgamsār* and *Nayacakrasār*.

The other poet in Bhimsingh Manak Sha's collection who in many ways is closest to Ānandghan in his spiritual emphasis is Banārsīdās. While one could argue that Banārsīdās—by his commitment to the non-sectarian Adhyātma movement which eventually was absorbed into the mainstream of north Indian Digambar spirituality (Lath 1981; Cort 2002b)—exhibited a similar emphasis on internal spiritual realities over external religious structures as did Ānandghan, the subsequent history of Banārsīdās and his writings is crucially central to north Indian Digambar self-identity in a way that is in striking contrast to the continuing problematic marginality of Ānandghan to Mūrtipūjak self-identity.

In other words, the family of poets posited by Bhimsingh Manak Sha helps us, in part, to locate Ānandghan within a mode of late-medieval Jain spirituality. At the same time, however, it confirms his status as an outsider to the mainstream ritual, institutional and devotional culture of the late-medieval Tapā Gaccha.

A third framework within which we can situate Ānandghan is one that has not hitherto been explored by scholars of Jainism, and may come as a surprise to some: the genre of his poems on Holi. This springtime festival has long been condemned by Jain intellectuals because it expresses values profoundly at odds with the cardinal Jain ethical imperative of *ahiṁsā*, non-harm. On the first evening of the festival, people in every village and neighbourhood in north India light giant bonfires and thus symbolically burn the demoness Holikā. From a Jain perspective, however, this is simply an act in which thousands of innocent lives are needlessly incinerated. Then the next morning people 'play Holi' with one another, throwing coloured liquids and powders on each other in a riotous carnival of abandonment. The consumption of intoxicating *bhāṅg* is also common on this day. All of this runs directly counter to a Jain emphasis on decorum, control, mindfulness and non-harm. Orthodox Jains therefore shun participation in this celebration of emotional abandon.

The celebration of Holi (or, in Braj pronunciation, Horī) is marked in north India by distinct poetic and musical performances. In many Hindu temples the festival starts days earlier with the singing of Holi songs. These are sung in a style unique to this season known as Phaguā, after the spring month of Phāgun. The cold weather of the winter has finally passed, and in traditional India this was also the time when husbands and wives looked forward to being reunited after the husband's time away from home working or soldiering. Phaguā also refers to *phāg*, the red powder people throw on one another on the morning of Holi, and therefore by extension to the festival itself. In north India the play of colours is associated most strongly with the love-play of Krishna and the *gopīs* in the Braj countryside. The artistic associations with the season are amplified by the widespread tradition of large public gatherings, known as *kavi-sammelans*, at which poets recite seasonal poems. While the Krishna theme of many of the poems is explicitly Hindu, the poets at these gatherings come from a wide array of religious communities. Muslim poets are well represented, and so one will equally find the poets referred to by the Arabic-derived word *śāyar* and the Sanskrit-derived word *kavi*. In the urbane, cosmopolitan culture of traditional urban north India, these musical and poetic gatherings are attended by everybody, including Jains.

But the Jains also have had their own counter-tradition of Holi songs. No. 24 in this volume is an example of such songs. In it Ānandghan refers metaphorically to the Holikā bonfire of the first evening. The destructive bonfire is equated with the painful burning of his mind due to separation from his beloved, and the resultant ashes, which are collected by people as sacred and healing residue, are equated with the poet's sense of disembodied confusion. This theme—of the unbearably painful separation from one's beloved—is a dominant theme of Holi songs. Ānandghan here allegorically spiritualizes the separation, for the beloved whom he misses is not Krishna or one of the gopīs, but Equanimity or Samatā, the grammatically feminine name for one of the prerequisites for advancing on the Jain path of liberation. It is rather turned upside down in Ānandghan, since Samatā (feminine noun) is longing for the human Soul or Consciousness (masculine nouns).

As the translators indicate in their introduction and notes, this use of abstract qualities and virtues as characters is widespread in Ānandghan's poetry. The main heroine of his allegorical poems is Sumati (Good Understanding or Right Belief), or sometimes Samatā. She is married to her husband Ātman (Self or Soul) or Cetan (Consciousness). If she is joined with him, all is well; but in the state of confusion created by *saṁsāra*, the couple is apart and so Soul lacks Right Belief. Nor is Soul in touch with Samatā (Equanimity) and Vivek (Discrimnation), two true spiritual friends. Instead, Soul runs after any of several women of ill repute: Kumati (Bad Understanding or Wrong Belief), Māyā (Illusion) and Mithyātva (Wrong Faith).

Ānandghan's poetry here fits into a long-standing Jain literary tradition of allegory (*rūpak*).[6] The earliest and most famous text in this genre is the *Upamiti-bhavaprapañcā Kathā* (The Story of the Development of Lives by Parable), a Sanskrit novel composed by the Śvetāmbar monk Siddharṣi in 906 CE. Every character in it serves a dual purpose: as an outward figure in the nominal

[6] For European-language introductions to the Jain genre of allegory see H. Jain 1962:9–24; and Balbir and Osier 2004:48–55.

drama itself, and an allegorical inner significance in the transit of the soul towards liberation. Siddharṣi termed this distinction *bahiraṅga* and *antaraṅga*, the outer limb and the inner limb.[7] Jain authors have returned to the genre throughout the centuries, although their compositions have been as influenced by the eleventh-century Brahmanical *Prabodhacandrodaya* (The Moonrise of Understanding) of Kṛṣṇamiśra as by Jain predecessors. In the late twelfth-century, Yaśaḥpāla, a Śvetāmbar Jain layman and minister in the Caulukya court, composed the *Moharājaparājaya* (The Defeat of King Delusion), a Sanskrit drama which ostensibly described Emperor Kumārapāla's conversion to Jainism by the monk Hemacandra, but on a deeper level conveyed the overcoming of spiritual delusion (*moha*). While it is quite possible, even likely, that Ānandghan knew Siddharṣi's novel, it is less likely that he knew of Yaśaḥpāla's drama itself. It is possible, however, that he knew of the allegorical story of the defeat of King Delusion. His contemporary Mānvijay, a disciple of Satvavijaygaṇi and a senior monastic associate of Yaśovijay who was active in the latter part of the seventeenth century, composed a Gujarati hymn to Mahāvīr, the *Moharājakathāgarbhit Vīrjinstavan* (Hymn to Mahāvīra Jina in Which Is Embedded the Story of King Delusion), in which he also narrated the story of King Delusion.[8]

Ānandghan in his allegorical poems, especially those in connection with Holi, might have been borrowing from a

[7] Peterson 1899:xviii.

[8] This hymn of either fifty-three or fifty-four verses has, to the best of my knowledge, not been published. According to Muni Jambūvijay's (1991:III:347) catalogue, there are two manuscripts of it in the Patan library. There may have been further connections between Ānandghan and Mānvijay, as the latter also composed a Gujarati *covīsī* or cycle of hymns to the twenty-four Jinas (Dośī 2006:109–18).

different Jain allegorical tradition. We have already seen that he most likely was influenced by Banārsīdās. Among this latter poet's Braj poems is the following one about Holi:[9]

Do the colour, let's go to the Jina's gate where the friends play Horī.
Right Belief and all her friends meet; they come and expel Wrong Belief.
Offer up the incense of saffron, sandalwood and perfume, the incense of the spirit of Equanimity.
Do the colour, let's go to the Jina's gate where the friends play Horī.
The sweets are compassion, the dried fruits are asceticism, the betel leaf is truth—chew all of it!
The eight karmas are tied in a rope and burnt in the fire of meditation.
Do the colour, let's go to the Jina's gate where the friends play Horī.
The drum plays the speech of the guru, the tambourine beats the rhythm of knowledge and forgiveness.
Banārsī says play this Horī and enjoy the city of liberation.
Do the colour, let's go to the Jina's gate where the friends play Horī.

This poem appears to have become one foundation of a long tradition, as Digambar poets over the next several centuries composed hundreds of songs that allegorized Holi. As the genre developed the characters became standardized. The cast in turn was based largely on another allegorical drama that was a Jain response to the *Prabodhacandrodaya*. This was the *Jñānasūryodaya* (The Sunrise of Knowledge), composed in 1591 CE in Sanskrit by Vādicandra, who was the Digambar *bhaṭṭārak*, landed pontiff of Mahuva in Gujarat.[10] The hero of the drama

[9] *Raṅga bhayo jina dvāra calo sakhi khelana horī*. Jain 1996:192.

[10] See the discussion of the drama by Hiralal Jain in his introduction to yet another allegorical work, the Apabhramsa *Madanaparājaya* of the Digambar Harideva (Jain 1962:13–17). Vādicandra composed another

was Ātman, who had two wives: a good wife Sumati and a bad wife Kumati. By each of them he had a number of sons, virtues born to Sumati and vices born to Kumati. Each side was further assisted by a number of virtuous and vicious allies. The allegory was borrowed by subsequent Digambar poets who composed their Holi poems in Braj and other north Indian vernaculars. They usually called the hero King Cetan, and made other modifications to fit the Holi theme.

There is no direct evidence that Ānandghan borrowed or even knew this Digambar allegorical genre. But, as we have seen, we know little else about him, and many of his poems appear to participate in the same allegorical milieu. It is possible, therefore, that he participated in the circles of Jain laymen and monks—some of them being Digambar circles, but more so the ecumenical gatherings that came to be known as Adhyātma or Spirituality—in the urban centres of northern India. These circles comprised of fellow seekers who met to discuss philosophy and spiritual realities, and to compose and sing pads. As the Adhyātma circles gradually were absorbed into the north Indian Digambar mainstream, Ānandghan continued to be a presence, and so we find pads by him in manuscript libraries connected to Digambar temples, and in modern printed anthologies of Digambar spiritual poems.

In the end Ānandghan remains a mystery to us in many ways. He clearly wanted it that way. A constant theme throughout his poetry is the necessity for each person to experience, for himself or herself, the spiritual realities of the inner soul. No one else can do it for us, not even a brilliant poet such as Ānandghan. The modern reader may want to know more about this poet. Like

---

Sanskrit text directly related to our theme, the *Holikācaritra* (Chaudhrī 1973:53). To the best of my knowledge neither of Vādicandra's texts has been published.

the Buddhist parable about not mistaking the finger pointing at the moon for the moon (enlightenment) itself, Ānandghan deflects attention from himself. He points us instead to the eternal truths of which he sang, in songs which Imre Bangha and R.C.C. Fynes have so eloquently translated for us.

John E. Cort
Denison University

Introduction

The Śvetāmbar ascetic Ānandghan, who was also known as Lābhānand, is one of the most popular Jain vernacular poets. Amongst the Jains of Gujarat and Rajasthan, he is respected not only as a poet but also as a great yogi—for centuries miraculous stories have been current about his yogic powers. Together with the merchant-poet Banārsīdās, the reformist leader Satyavijay and the philosopher Yaśovijay he was one of the people who most markedly shaped seventeenth-century Jainism in north India, and his oeuvre still remains an active force.

His poetry is highly praised by scholars, his hymns to the fordmakers are sung in Jain communities even outside India,[1] and his songs are popular amongst a diverse array of devotees. Moreover, his songs are not restricted to Jain themes; with their powerful imagery they awaken in any listener a desire to search for the transcendental. Their universal appeal inspired Mahatma Gandhi to include one of Ānandghan's poems (No. 35 in our edition) in his prayer book, the *Āśram Bhajanāvalī*.

[1] In October 2002 Mr Jayeshbhai Shah at the Jain Temple in Leicester in Britain stated that their worship included some of Ānandghan's hymns.

The poetry translated here, therefore, is not simply an exposition of Jainism; it also has a more universal message. Although Ānandghan's Jain identity cannot be questioned, he is by no means sectarian. Just as during his life as a wandering ascetic Ānandghan communicated with people who were not necessarily Jains, similarly today one does not need to confine oneself to a Jain point of view to be able to appreciate these poems fully. Although he often refers to Jain concepts, Ānandghan is never intent on establishing the supremacy of Jain tenets over those of another religion. He declares again and again that these differences are but superficial in comparison with the inner experience on the path towards the Absolute. In manuscript collections, his songs were often entitled adhyātma pad or 'transcendental songs'. Ānandghan does not indulge in speculations on the nature of the transcendent: his aim is rather to provide the stimulus to undertake a journey towards it. His poems are replete with strikingly fresh imagery with the intention of awakening his audience to the realization that they have a task to fulfil in the world and that they should not forget about the transcendental dimensions of their lives amidst the everyday struggles of material existence. As he advocates this higher consciousness, the world that surrounds him springs into life in the metaphors of his songs. The world of his poems is populated with merchants, ascetics, watchmen, bombardiers, showmen, gurus, disciples, women with wounded pride, and above all, with the most popular erotic and transcendental theme of his times, that of women longing for their absent lover.

Ānandghan's Life

Legends

As is the case with most early modern poets of India, the life of Ānandghan is enshrouded in legends and there are only a few facts that are definitely known about him.

Present-day readers often find that information about the life and times of a poet helps to heighten their appreciation of his or her poetry. However, in early-modern India it was not the factual details of the lives of poets and saints that their audience was interested in and this subsequently transmitted to later generations. As a consequence there is a lack of biographical data that can be the cause of frustration for the modern researcher. Yet there exists an ample body of traditional material about the lives of poets and saints from which references to their actual lives can be extracted; however, this material is more useful in providing an understanding of how the poets were regarded in earlier times. Stories that relate the miraculous deeds of Ānandghan and his near contemporaries were manifestations of their advanced spiritual achievements and also attest the popularity of tantric practices in Rajasthan. Although Jainism did not produce a full-scale alternative tantric path to liberation, certain aspects of tantra, such as the use of magic spells, mantras and magical designs, yantras that cure diseases, provide material wealth or defeat enemies, had been absorbed into Jainism by Ānandghan's time.[2] The legends concerning Ānandghan and his contemporaries—collected in the first half of the twentieth century and presumably dating back to the nineteenth century or earlier—were described in detail by Buddhisagarsuri,[3] Ānandghan's first modern biographer. These stories present the poet as a great yogi who participated in the social life of his times and who attained *siddhi*s, miraculous yogic powers, often associated with stereotypical miracles that are ascribed also to other saints. It is his asceticism that earned him the epithet *yogīrāj*, 'king of the yogis'. On the other hand, there are a few passages that show him in a less favourable

[2] Cort 2000, Dundas 2000 and Cort 2000b.

[3] Buddhisagar pp. 183–197 and Kharaid pp. 75–86. For a rationalist take on these legends see Bhamvarlal Nahta pp. xiii–xvii.

light—as one who is a formidable miracle-worker but whose transcendental knowledge is defective. These legends, whether showing Ānandghan in a favourable or unfavourable light, are all in agreement to the fact that he had extraordinary yogic powers. This is all the more interesting because the stories about Ānandghan's miraculous powers often provide a very different picture from the one that is presented in his poetry. In fact, only a few of his poems can be associated even somewhat remotely with the popular legends about him: for instance, the ones featuring a woman with wounded pride and the story of the conciliation of a queen with the king.

Most stories present Ānandghan in a favourable light. There are, however, legends which do not show him as a person to be followed or admired. For example, in the account of his defeat in a philosophical contest at the hands of Prāṇlāl he is presented in an adverse sectarian light. The tantric fight at the end of this story is a stock expression of a struggle for sectarian dominance.[4]

This legend is mentioned in the *Bītak* (verses 33, 42–7)[5] a sectarian biography of Prāṇlāl composed by Lāldās in 1694. The same information is found in another work, the *Nijānand Caritāmṛt*, apparently a prose reworking of the *Bītak*:[6]

> Prāṇlāl left Pālanpur and teaching on his way he arrived [at] the town of Merta. In this place lived an ascetic called Lābhānand and he struck up a discussion with Prāṇlāl. He had great skills in yoga and miracle-working. He spent about ten days with Prāṇlāl in discussing transcendental wisdom. When eventually he was defeated he grew very angry with Prāṇlāl. With the use of magic spells and

[4] Cf. Dundas 2000 p. 235.

[5] Sharma 1965. See Desai 1998 pp. 50–1.

[6] Śāstrī, Kṛṣṇadatt: *Nijānand Caritāmṛt* pp. 518–19. Quoted in Desai 1998 pp. 49–50.

incantations he lifted up stones and hills and started to throw them on Prāṇlāl. He performed a lot of witchcraft but none of it had any effect on Prāṇlāl. Giving up hope, finally Lābhānand had to stop, thereby admitting defeat.

Name

The poet today is known by two names. His sectarian name, which he received after initiation, was Lābhānand. In his poetry, however, he used Ānandghan as a poetic signature, the name by which he has been widely known. The compound word 'ānand-ghan' means 'cloud of bliss', that is, 'source of bliss' or 'extensive bliss'. A remarkable aspect of the name is that it lacks any sectarian connotation and people bearing it are known to have belonged to different sects and even to different religions. Although it is a rare name, several people named Ānandghan were involved in literary activity.

The confusion surrounding the name of the Jain Ānandghan is further complicated by the fact that a Jain commentator on his works, Jñānsār (1744–1841), followed by the Bengali scholar Kṣitimohan Sen,[7] attempted to conflate the figure of the Nimbārkī Ānandghan[8] with that of the Jain Ānandghan. However, the research of Vishvanath Prasad Mishra has clearly demonstrated that the two poets were not identical.[9]

Dating

The dating given by scholars to Ānandghan is not beyond dispute. However, because of Ānandghan's connection with the

[7] Agarchand Nahta 1974 p. 27 and Sen pp. 3–11.

[8] On the Nimbārkī Ānandghan see Bangha 1999.

[9] Mishra 1952 'Vāṅmukh' pp. 53–55.

prolific writer Yaśovijay, it seems reasonable to accept that he lived in the seventeenth century. Yaśovijay wrote an *Aṣṭapadī*, a poem in eight stanzas, in praise of Ānandghan.[10] Yaśovijay's poem and the following verse by Ānandghan (No. 51) suggest that the two poets knew each other well.

Oh Jas, listen to what I say: if I find this, then my wandering is averted!
How shall I meet my stainless friend?

Umravchand Jargad and Agarchand Nahta[11] interpret 'Jas' as a reference to Yaśovijay, whose poetic signature, *chāp*, was Yaś or Jas. The word 'jas', however, is not necessarily a name and can simply mean 'as', giving the translation 'Listen to the words as says Ānandghan'. Moreover, the poem is not represented in any of the manuscripts surveyed by Jargad. Buddhisagarsuri, who discovered it, did not indicate its provenance. Despite these reservations, there is some reason to believe that the two great authors did indeed know each other, and, if we may judge from the deference shown him in Yaśovijay's *Aṣṭapadī*, Ānandghan was Yaśovijay's senior. Recent scholarly consensus puts the dates of Yaśovijay as 1624–1688.[12] One can, therefore, surmise that Ānandghan was born before 1624.

In their introduction to their critical edition of Ānandghan's poems, the *Ānandghan Granthāvalī*, Umravchand Jargad and

[10] This *Aṣṭapadī* is published in several places e.g. Mishra 1945 pp. 331–332; Kharaid pp. 11–13; Buddhisagar pp. 164–165.

[11] Kharaid p. 243 and Agarchand Nahta 1974 p. 20.

[12] Hiralal Kapariya, *Yaśodohan*. Śri Yaśobhāratī Prakāśan Samiti, Bombay, 1966; Pradyumnavijayagani, Jayant Kothari and Kantibhai Shah (eds), *Upādhyāy Yaśovijay Svādhyāy Granth*. Śrī Mahāvīr Jain Vidyālay, Bombay, 1993; Darshana Kothari and Dipti Shah (eds), *Upādhyāy Śrī Yaśovijay Sāhitya Sūci*. Śrutajñān Prasārak Sabhā, Ahmedabad, 1999.

Mahtab Chandra Kharaid gave the date of Ānandghan's death as 1674. Their argument was based on the assertion of an ascetic of the Praṇāmī sect who saw a book called *Prāṇlāl jī Mahārāj kā Jīvan Caritra*, a description of the life of Prāṇlāl (1618–94), the founder of the sect. According to Jargad and Kharaid, the book stated that Prāṇlāl went to Merta in 1674, where he met Ānandghan alias Lābhānand. In that very same year Ānandghan died. This book may be no other than the *Bītak* mentioned earlier, in which verses 33,42–47 describe this event. According to Jargad and Kharaid, the same information is found in another work, the *Nijānand Caritāmṛt*,[13] which seems to be a prose reworking of the *Bītak*.[14] Desai, however, has observed that neither of these Praṇāmī works contains any reference to Prāṇlāl's return to Merta a year later to find Ānandghan dead.[15] Moreover, both are sectarian works which relate miraculous events, and attempts to extrapolate historical information from them must be viewed with caution.

A Jain Gujarati text, *Śrī Sametśikhar Tīrthanāṁ Dhāliyāṁ*, written around the first half of the nineteenth century, mentions Lābhānand as the younger brother of Satyavijay Paṁnyās, a famous ascetic of the Tapāgaccha lineage, who, disillusioned with factionalism, refused to accept the religious leadership of the Tapāgaccha and started the *saṁvegī* lineage, from which almost all contemporary Tapāgaccha monks claim their descent.[16] Based on this Desai stated that Ānandghan must have lived sometime between 1599 and 1699. However, the text in

[13] Kharaid p. 14.

[14] The passage describing Prāṇlāl's meeting with Ānandghan in this work has been given in translation in the 'Legends' section on pages xvi–xvii.

[15] Desai 1998 pp. 49–51.

[16] Desai 1998 pp. 13, 21–25. On Satyavijay, see Cort 2000a and Cort 2001, p. 44 (and note).

which this evidence is given was written much later than the time of Ānandghan. A further reason for treating this evidence with caution is that the attempt to associate famous people who may not have had any actual contact with each other is a frequent literary topos in Indian hagiography. Whether the expression 'younger brother' here means biological brother or simply *guru-bhāī*, co-disciple, establishing the connection with Satyavijay can be seen as a way of linking Ānandghan to someone seen as the most important reformer of the times.

Manuscripts, rather than hagiography, can provide more reliable evidence for the dating of Ānandghan. In the colophons of handwritten books, scribes have often noted the dates when they finished the copying. The oldest available manuscript of Ānandghan's twenty-two *stavana*s, hymns, was copied in 1694.[17] Since this is in all probability his last work, unfinished at the time of his death, we may surmise that by that date Ānandghan was dead.

On the basis of the evidence discussed above, we are able to accept that Ānandghan was born some time before 1624 and died before 1694.

Language and Place

The language of Ānandghan's other major work, his twenty-four (actually twenty-two) hymns, is different from that of his songs. The *Caubīsī* is written in a mixture of Rajasthani and Gujarati, while the songs are close to the Hindi of the Sant-poets and to Brajbhāṣā, the most popular literary dialect of mid-sixteenth to mid-nineteenth century north India, with the addition of some Rajasthani-Gujarati vocabulary. Rajasthani—which, although

[17] Desai 1980 pp. 152–155.

sometimes considered as a group of Hindi dialects, has recently been categorized as one of the official languages of India—is in certain dialects closer to Gujarati than to Hindi and was even closer in the seventeenth century. Therefore, attempting to distinguish between the two languages is not always fruitful, especially not in the case of a text that presents features from both. According to the Gujarati scholar Kumarpal Desai, the hymns' language leans more towards Rajasthani than towards Gujarati. However, he notes that the language of a wandering ascetic is a mixture of different dialects so that it can be widely understood; hence, it does not help in determining his place of origin and chief place of residence.[18]

As far as Ānandghan's birthplace is concerned, if one accepts the reference of the *Śrī Sametśikhar Tīrthanāṁ Dhāliyāṁ* to Lābhānand as the younger brother of Satyavijay Paṁnyās, then we can surmise that Ānandghan was born in the same place as he. Satyavijay Paṁnyās was born in Malwa but spent most of his life in Rajasthan. According to Kumarpal Desai, Ānandghan also left Malwa for Rajasthan[19] since the legends quoted earlier connect Ānandghan with Mount Abu, Jodhpur and Merta in Rajasthan. His connection to Merta is also indicated by a Jain shrine in the town that is today called *Ānandghanjī kā Upāśray*, Ānandghan's Shelter.[20]

Ānandghan's Works

As has been mentioned earlier, two collections of poems, the *Caubīsī* ('Collection of Twenty-four') and the *Bahattarī*

[18] Desai 1998 p. 26.
[19] Desai 1998 p. 27.
[20] Desai 1998 p. 48.

('Collection of Seventy-two') are ascribed to Ānandghan. Apart from these collections, some stray songs and a Sanskrit work consisting of twenty-four verse couplets have been found in manuscripts.

The Ānandghan-Caubīsī

The smaller collection of Ānandghan's poems, the *Caubīsī*, consists of twenty-four hymns, one to each of the twenty-four Jain Tīrthaṅkaras, the spiritual fordmakers. The preparation of 'collections of twenty-four' is a long-standing Jain tradition that includes such works as Mānvijay's *Stavan-caubīsī* and Rāmvijay's *Caubīsī* on devotion and knowledge.[21] Another caubīsī associated with *adhyātmik* strands of image-worshipping spirituality is that of Devcandra.[22]

As with most of Ānandghan's other works, the stavanas are in the pad form with refrain and attribution to a raga. However, the last two hymns in the collection were not written by Ānandghan, and the work may have originally been called *Ānandghan-bāvīsī* ('Collection of Twenty-two'). Its critical edition, based on four manuscripts copied between 1694 and 1718, was prepared by Kumarpal Desai.[23] Desai lists 174 manuscripts of the collection prepared in the eighteenth and nineteenth centuries, thus providing an attestation that it was one of the most frequently copied books of early modern Jainism.

There are three attested early commentaries on the work, out of which only two are extant and the earliest one, prepared by Yaśovijay, is lost. All commentators mention twenty-two

[21] Desai 1998 pp. 99–100.

[22] This was recently re-edited by Kantibhai B. Shah and published by Śrī Śrutajñān Prasārak Sabhā, Ahmedabad, 2003.

[23] Desai 1980 pp. 152–297.

hymns of Ānandghan only. However, it seems that the authors of the two extant commentaries completed the collection of twenty-four stavanas, adding the last two hymns with the poetic signature 'Ānandghan'—one for each of the remaining two fordmakers, Pārśvanātha and Mahāvīra—to the collection on which they were preparing a commentary. The fact that each of the two extant commentaries contain completely different versions of the two final hymns supports this interpretation.

There is a legend concerning the composition of the twenty-two hymns that tells how Yaśovijay accompanied by Jñānvimalsūri and other monks once went to search for Ānandghan in the temples on Mount Abu. They found him in one of the temples absorbed in singing the praises of the twenty-four Tīrthaṅkaras. Everyone was silently listening to Ānandghan. Yaśovijay's memory was so sharp that, once he had heard, he did not forget what Ānandghan had uttered. When Ānandghan finished the twenty-two hymns and was about to start the praise of Pārśvanātha, he heard a noise and turned around. As soon as he saw Yaśovijay, he stopped singing and went to greet him.[24]

Although we have rich early manuscript material for the stavanas, both this legend and the pad verse form, characteristic of sung poetry, show that these hymns were originally composed for singing and were transmitted orally.

The Ānandghan-Bahattarī

The other collection, the *Bahattarī*, 'Collection of Seventy-two', is a collection of Ānandghan's pads. Although the number

[24] Kharaid p. 79; Bhamvarlal Nahta p. xiv. Buddhisagarsuri connects this story not with Mount Abu but with the Shatrunjaya Hill (see Buddhisagar pp. 196–7 and Kharaid pp. 9–10).

of poems in the manuscripts is more than seventy-two, this is the closest traditional Indian round number to the number of songs in the earliest form of this collection. The songs in it are not confined to Jain themes. They are concerned with devotion, renunciation, general wisdom, yoga, love, pangs of separation (*virah*), transcendental spiritualism (adhyātma), philosophy and other topics.

The Songs

The most widely used genres of medieval Hindi devotional poetry were the verse couplets (*dohās*) and the songs with a refrain (pads). While the brief dohā can be highly persuasive, it also tends to be hortatory. The longer pad is, by its nature, more flexible, less emphatic and able to give greater scope to emotions, even when expounding philosophical ideas.

Both couplets and songs are written in quantitative or moraic metres based on the length of time taken to pronounce each syllable: a short syllable counts as one metrical unit or *mora* and a long syllable counts as two. The word stress is also important. A pause or caesura usually divides the line into two slightly unequal sections. The caesura often marks the separation of two syntactic units, such as clauses or independent sentences. The number of moraic units is fixed in each half line. For example, the following line in *sār* metre has sixteen units in its first half. There are a further twelve in its concluding half, and each of the two rhyming syllables (*-ve kā*) is long.

saba mili hota barābara lekhā, iha viveka giṇave kā.
11 11 2 1 1 2 1 1 2 2| 1 1 1 2 1 1 2 2 2|
Adding all together the amount is equal; this is the science of calculation.

This rhythm peculiar to medieval Hindi cannot be reproduced in English translation.

The verses rhyme with at least two rhyming syllables. The same rhyme may continue throughout the poem or each two-lined unit may have a rhyme differing from the other units. The only element of the verse that we reproduce in the translation is the division of the line into halves. Songs usually begin with the refrain, which is called *ṭek* in the manuscripts, but some pads have an introductory dohā couplet before the refrain.

Ānandghan was not the first Jain to compose pads. Poets such as Kumudcand (fl. 1588)[25] and Banārsīdās (1586–1643) had previously used this form. Nevertheless, judging from the high number of manuscripts of Ānandghan's songs, he was one of the most successful Jain masters of the genre.

Imagery and Philosophy

Jain ascetics—yatis and sādhus, for the most part—did not have a fixed abode in monasteries, although the former tended to spend more time in one place than the latter.[26] For eight months of the year they travelled continuously, often with itineraries set months and even years in advance, mainly in Gujarat and Rajasthan, where there is a substantial Jain population. It was only the four months of the rainy season, the Caumāsā, when it was impossible to travel, that they remained in a monastery. Continuous travel exposed them to the influences of the linguistic and religious diversity of India. They mixed with Vaishnava and Shaiva mendicants, with Muslim Sufi mystics, with the followers of Kabīr and Dādū as well as with Sikhs. They

[25] Sharma and Snatak 1974 p. 455.

[26] Desai 1980 pp. 152–297. See also Cort 1991.

also must have had contacts with professional singers of dynastic histories and heroic songs, the *cāraṇ*s and *bhāṭ*s. The interaction, however, was not one-sided. They not only received influences from other sects and religions but also sang poetry to a wider, not necessarily Jain, public.

Rather than sophisticated philosophical argumentation incomprehensible to the masses, Ānandghan used powerful imagery with metaphors and similes familiar to ordinary people. The largest part of Ānandghan's imagery is shared with the imagery of devotional songs and the imagery of the Hindi court poetry of his times. This imagery, however, can be reinvested with a Jain spiritual meaning.

In Indian devotional poetry the imagery of mundane love is used to express the individual's longing for the transcendental. In Krishna poetry, a feminine voice, usually that of a cowherd woman longing for Krishna, is heard. Her most frequent theme is love and the pangs of separation from her lover, called virah in Hindi. In contrast to this feminine viewpoint, Muslim Sufi poetry uses a masculine voice. Here, God is symbolized by an apparently unattainable woman. One of the major themes of seventeenth- and eighteenth-century Hindi court-poetry and art is that of the *nāyikā-bhed*, the description of the heroine and the effects of love upon her in the different stages of love. So we encounter women, who have fallen in love at first glance and are eager to meet their lover, women whose husbands are abroad or women with wounded pride, *khaṇḍitā*s, whose lover has been unfaithful.

One of the central themes of love-poetry is virah, the pangs of separation. The fact that the names of both Ānandghan and the most celebrated medieval exponent of virah, Mīrā Bāī, are associated with the town of Merta in Rajasthan may simply be a coincidence. The similarity of their themes, however, certainly attests the popularity of virah songs in the region. Their popularity in Rajasthan most probably reflects a social reality in which men were away from home for long periods either on trade journeys or for the performance of military service for wealthy employers.[27]

Ānandghan's characters are animated by the intensity of their feelings, either on the plane of love or on the transcendental plane of the urge to turn towards the Absolute. In accordance with the popular convention in both court and religious poetry in Rajasthan during his time, a female voice is often heard in Ānandghan's songs. However, the poet is unconventional in his use of traditional themes of love lyrics. In contrast with Krishna poetry, the personified voice evoked by Ānandghan is not that of the soul longing for the Absolute. Heroes and heroines are vehicles of various abstractions such as Equanimity, the Self, Illusion etc. The love-lorn woman in the songs is generally the personified Sumati (Good Understanding) or Samatā (Equanimity), meaning, in the Jain context, the detachment of one's consciousness from all external objects.[28] Her husband or lover is Cetan (Consciousness), or Ātman (the Self). Although their love is founded on immediate understanding and there is consequently no need for go-betweens, there can be a friend—Śraddhā (Faith or Veneration) or Anubhav (Experience)—whom Samatā frequently addresses. As described in the Foreword, this use of a stock set of allegorical characters predated Ānandghan by at least some decades and remained popular until the nineteenth century. It must have been easily understood by most of Ānandghan's listeners and readers as is also clear from later commentaries. Jñānsār—whose commentary

[27] Kolff 1990 pp. 74–84.

[28] On the attainment of equanimity see Jaini 1998 pp. 221–6 and for a short survey of the use of equanimity in Jain literature see Sudarshanashri pp. 240–241.

on the *Bāvīsī*, Ānandghan's original collection of hymns to the fordmakers, was written in 1809—also commented on sixteen of Ānandghan's pads. An example of his interpretation is given below.[29] The commentary relates to song No. 24 in our collection:

Without my lover I forgot good sense.

I swing with my eyes fixed on the window of the palace of grief.
Without my lover I forgot good sense.

I laughed seeing other women wasting away in body and mind.
But when I understood, I said only 'Nobody should fall in love!'
Without my lover I forgot good sense.

'How can I live without my lover, the dearest lord of my life?'
The snakes of separation drink up the breath of life.
Without my lover I forgot good sense.

Why apply a cool fan, saffron or sandalwood paste?
This is not a fire but a fire of separation; they increase the burning of the body.
Without my lover I forgot good sense.

The bonfire of the Holi festival is lit with songs one night in spring.
My mind is burning every day and the ashes of my body are scattered by the wind.
Without my lover I forgot good sense.

Come to my palace, Equanimity, and give the juice of your voice.
I'm at your service, lord, Cloud of Bliss. How can you be so cruel?
Without my lover I forgot good sense.

[29] Nahta, Agarchand (ed.): *Jñānsār Padāvalī*. p. 236. Quoted in Kharaid pp. 56–59.

Jñānsār explains that in this poem Sumati, or Samatā, speaks to her friend, Śraddhā. The absent lover is Ātman, whose separation from Sumati/Samatā due to involvement with other women means that he has indulged in impurities. The application of cool materials is *yathāpravṛttikaraṇa* 'acting in accordance with entry (onto the path)'—i.e. the soul's impulse to cultivate the religious life—and after this *apūrvakaraṇa* 'bringing about an unprecedented state—of diminution of karmic accretion' will come, in which the knot of passion and anger is solved. In the subsequent *anavṛttikaraṇa* there will be union with the Self, which means the attainment of *samyakatva*, 'the true state'. The burning of the body and mind means that the pure form of 'good understanding' had been immolated and had become 'bad understanding'. If the lover comes, then 'understanding' will become 'good understanding'. One should, therefore, not indulge in impurities.

An image frequently found in Jain poetry—one already used by the Jain writer Banārsīdās in the first half of the seventeenth century—is the contrast between *samatā* with *mamatā*. After Ānandghan, poets such as Yaśovijay, Jñānsār or Rājcandra referred to 'Equanimity' as the only way towards the Absolute. The tradition of personifying *sumati* was also continued by Yaśovijay, who wrote poems using the imagery of the separation of Good Understanding from her lover, the Self.

Ānandghan's pool of imagery is deep and it includes metaphors such as that of the four-sided chess, the *caupaṛa*, which is a game played with an oblong dice on a cloth or board with a cross-shaped layout. Despite its apparent originality, this image is also found in a song attributed to the most famous Krishna-poet, Sūrdās '*caupari jagata maḍe juga bīte . . .*'[30] Both poems compare

[30] *Sūrsāgar* 60 in Vājpeyī 1952 Vol. I. p. 20.

life to the game of caupaṛa and describe the workings of māyā, Illusion. There is, however, a marked difference in the treatment of the theme. While the poem attributed to Sūrdās abounds in numbers embedded with esoteric meanings, Ānandghan's song uses a plethora of images. Moreover, Ānandghan's song has an optimistic conclusion in contrast with the pessimism shown in the final line of the poem in the *Sūrsāgar*, which reads:

sūra eka pau nāma binā nara phiri phiri bājī hārī.
Sūrdās says, without the only ace, God's name, man again and again has lost the game.

The final line of Ānandghan's poem is:

ānandaghana prabhu pāva dikhāvata, to jītai jīva gājī.
When the lord, the cloud of bliss, shows an ace, then does the soul triumphantly win.

This is not the only instance that a theme is common in both Ānandghan and another poet. The theme of the spinning wheel is also shared with some early modern Sufi poems.[31]

The poem from which the title of this book is taken likens the world to a showman's creation of illusion. Here Ānandghan's choice of words strikes a chord with which each of his listeners would have been familiar. The compound word translated as city-showman is *naṭnāgar*, the word *naṭ* meaning 'dancer, acrobat, showman' and *nāgar*, 'urbane' that is 'skilled', 'clever'.

[31] See the chapter 'The Sufis as Literati' and especially its sub-chapter 'The Literati and Their Popular Literature' in Eaton 1978 pp. 155–164. An example of a *carkhā* song is Bulhe Shah: *Merā eh naulakhā rakhā kuṛe* sung by Nusrat Fateh Ali Khan (Cassette 'Royal' No. 532, Vol. 9, A1). Imre Bangha has received a transcription and a French translation of this song from Denis Matringe.

When this compound occurs in Krishna poetry, it is used by the cowherd women to refer to Krishna to evoke the sense that he is originally not from their world and that they may not always be able to comprehend his actions.

Some songs use an imagery infrequently found in other religious songs. For instance, one poem addresses a watchman who indicates worldly time by striking a bell, while another describes the human being as a wagon speeding out of control which is eventually looted. Others express the plight of a woman who had been married off to a mere child.

Classical Jain philosophy does not accept the notion of God as ultimate reality. However, one of the most commonly used terms to designate the transmigrating soul (*jīva*) in its pure unconditioned form is *paramātman*, which has come to be regarded as an object of veneration. This divine principle, sometimes referred to as God, exists in a potential state within all beings.[32] The purely conscious form (*caitanya svarūpa*) of the transmigrating soul and of the supreme god are similar. In Ānandghan's time, the veneration of God in Jainism was intensified by the influence received from popular Hindi devotional poetry, especially that of the so-called Nirgun Sants, such as Raidās, Kabīr or Dādū Dayāl, who worshipped an untainted (*nirañjan*) deity beyond qualities (*guṇas*). This approach was close to the Jain *adhyātmavāda*, a highly immanent, internal spirituality, propagated by Banārsīdās (1586–1643).[33] Adhyātmavāda was continued within the Digambar lineage by dozens of poets, almost all of them householders like Dyānatrāy (1676–1727).[34] Its use was less prominent within the Śvetāmbar

[32] Dundas p. 94.

[33] Buddhisagar p. 151; Nahta pp. x–xi.

[34] On Dyānatrāy and on the performance of Jain Bhakti songs see Cort (forthcoming).

tradition.[35] It is, therefore, not a surprise that pads by Ānandghan do appear in Digambar collections.[36]

The acceptance of God, who is 'the cloud of bliss' is by no means the only one of Ānandghan's themes that is influenced by the Nirgun Sants. Other meeting points include the superiority of internal experience over learning, descriptions of the workings of māyā, the consciousness of the closeness of death and the consequent exhortation to use one's time to strive towards the final goal of life.

In spite of Ānandghan's reputation as a great yogi, explicit references to *haṭhayoga* or *rājayoga* terminology are rare.[37] Ānandghan's emphasis is on the yogic inner experience, the *anubhava*. His is a religion based more on inner experience than on transmitted knowledge. This is all the more noteworthy since at his time affiliation to a guru was pivotal irrespective of sect. Ānandghan stresses the importance of experience over that of the spiritual master—'The world is my guru and I am the disciple of the world'—and he exalts 'the flower of the experience of the Self'.

Due to the closeness of some of their pivotal themes, there are several songs that have been attributed to both Ānandghan and Kabīr,[38] the most prominent representative of the Sants and one of the most celebrated poets of Hindi. Twentieth-century scholars sometimes refer to Ānandghan as the Jain Kabīr.

[35] See Foreword and also Dundas pp. 94, 204.

[36] See Foreword.

[37] Reference to yogic posture and the wordless prayer is present in only one of our translated songs (No. 8). Another song, *Padāvalī* 75 (not included in this volume) uses terms such as *īḍā*, *piṅgalā*, *suṣumnā*, *brahmarandhra*, *anāhata nāda*, *yama*, *niyama*, *āsana* etc.

[38] Agarchand Nahta 1978; Agarchand Nahta 1974 pp. 35–36; Kharaid p. 226.

Naturally, there is some explicitly Jain imagery in Ānandghan's songs. For instance, the poem in praise of Pārśvanātha, the twenty-third fordmaker, contains references to a well-known legend about him.[39] Starting with a description of the rains in the conventional style, the song recounts the demon Meghamālin's attempt to destroy Pārśva with rain from thunder clouds, even as the fordmaker remained rapt in meditation. But when the flood reached his nose the king of the snakes came and protected him with his coils and hood, his *pārśva.*

Some poems not included in the *Bahattarī* are called *sajjhāys*, study. Sajjhāy (Sanskrit: *svādhyāya*, self-recitation) was originally counted among the six internal ascetic practices, *tapaścaryā.* Poems intended to support this practice were also called sajjhāys. They are illustrative stories in verse by which a mendicant can learn the basics of any topic: metaphysics, soteriology, history, etc. In the more conservative circles of the Tapāgaccha, they are particularly the province of the nuns, who are forbidden to study many of the scriptures.

Two sajjhāys were found by Agarchand Nahta,[40] while one *Ātmopadeś Sajjhāy* composed in a language close to modern Gujarati has been published by Desai. Although it has the poetic signature of Ānandghan, Desai admits that on linguistic grounds it does not seem to be a poem by our poet. Another *Ātmabodh Sajjhāy*, this time in a language close to the Khaṛī Bolī dialect of modern Hindi, can be found in a manuscript

[39] Some aspects of this legend are shared with Buddhism. But, by the time of Ānandghan, the imagery was more widely known in connection with Pārśvanāth than with the Buddha. In the Buddhist version the nāga Mucilinda protected the Buddha against the heavy monsoon showers that fell after his enlightenment by spreading his hood over the head of the Enlightened One.

[40] Nahta 1974 pp. 37–38, 40.

copied in 1825.[41] This poem is included in our selection as an example of this genre.

According to the commentators, one of the underlying themes of Jain philosophy present in Ānandghan's poems is the doctrine of many-pointedness (*anekāntavāda*). Probably having its origins in the idea of the fordmakers' omniscience, which enables them to see things from various perspectives, the doctrine of many-pointedness has been discussed in the works of Hemacandra and Haribhadra, and has become one of the defining features of Jainism. According to this doctrine, things should be looked at from the seven logical standpoints (*naya*s) through which judgements can be made. These standpoints are the figurative (*naigama*), the collective (*saṅgraha*), the practical (*vyavahāra*), the momentary (*ṛjusūtra*), the verbal (*śabda*), the specific (*samabhirūḍha*) and the qualifying (*evambhūta*) standpoints.

According to the 'Theory of Maybe' (*syādvāda*), the seven viewpoints of this logic are:

1. In some respects it exists (*syāt asti*).
2. In some respects it does not exist (syāt *nāsti*).
3. In some respects it exists, and in some respects it does not exist (syāt asti nāsti).
4. In some respects it is inexpressible (syāt *avaktavya*).
5. In some respects it exists and is inexpressible (syāt asti avaktavya).
6. In some respects it does not exist and is inexpressible' (syāt nāsti avaktavya).
7. In some respects it exists, and in some respects it does not exist, and is inexpressible (syāt asti nāsti avaktavya).[42]

[41] Rajasthani Research Institute, Chopasni, No. 11634 ff. 23v–24r.
[42] Dundas pp. 197–200.

Though Ānandghan does not try to force the details of this doctrine into his poetry, one of his poems contains a reference to this system:

Is, is not, not in words, unreachable to senses;
is this evidenced by the standpoints, and the sevenfold?
Some exceptional unprejudiced one recognizes it—how could opinion-warriors see?

The Life of the Songs: Progressing on the Spiritual Path

The publication of these poems in the form of a book prompts the reader to read them as we now read the classics of Western poetry—silently, for our internal appreciation. However, we should bear in mind that literary culture in early modern India was at least as much an oral culture as it was a written one, being communicated and received by a wide range of means. At their birth these lyrics were sung and an audience listened to them and probably joined in the singing of the refrains. The original purpose of these songs was not the creation of aesthetic delight but rather *upāsnā*, a means to reach towards the transcendental. Singing, reciting, listening to, writing or reading these songs became—and for many still remains—a vehicle for advancement on the spiritual path.

Although we can conceive of these poems as lyrics to songs, they were not only transmitted orally. Soon after their composition some poems were written down and ever larger handwritten collections of Ānandghan's songs were prepared. The number of collected poems grew further with the advent of printing in the nineteenth century. Manuscript culture and print culture, however, did not suppress orality, and a combination of written and oral transmission continues to survive in India, where singers of traditional songs may learn their material not only from teachers but also from books.

A way of infusing continued life into the text was the preparation of written commentaries on the verses. The commentaries probably originate in oral discourses on the sometimes complicated symbolism of the poems. Many of the *Bāvīsī/Caubīsī* manuscripts also contain commentaries. Soon after Ānandghan's death the monk-scholar Yaśovijay apparently wrote a commentary entitled *Ānandghan-bāvīsī Bālāvabodh*, which, however, cannot be found today.[43] Fortunately, two other well-known old commentaries are still extant. In 1712 Jñānvimalsūri wrote a *bālāvabodh*, that is a vernacular commentary to the hymns.[44] The other one was prepared in 1809 by a scholar called Jñānsār, who also commented on some of the pads and made the statement about his work:

> I started to contemplate Ānandghan's hymns as early as 1829 of the Vikrama Era (1772 AD). The contemplation went on for 37 years. I have sought information from many people but I didn't get satisfaction. Eventually I saw that old age was approaching and when I spent the four months of the rainy season of 1866 of the Vikrama Era (1809 AD) in Kishangarh I wrote a vernacular commentary on Ānandghan's twenty-two hymns.[45]

Although relatively less commentarial material was prepared on the pads than on the hymns, Jñānsār's statement attests the

[43] The title of this commentary appears in a list of Yaśovijay's works dating from 1710. See Agarchand Nahta 1947 p. 231.
[44] Bhamvarlal Nahta *Prakāśakīy* p. 1.
[45] Agarchand Nahta pp. 25–26. The Hindi text given by Nahta seems to be corrupt saying 'he wrote'.

extraordinary extent of human effort that could be spent on the preparation of a commentary.

Performance

The most conspicuous peculiarity of the pad is that it can be divided into a refrain of one or two lines and a verse that usually consists of two to ten lines. There is a marked difference between text and performance. In sung performance, the refrain called *dhruva*, or *sthāyī* (both meaning 'constant' or 'permanent'), is repeated several times at the beginning and, usually, after every second line. In this way it separates the verse into two-lined strophes, and the content of these strophes tends to be more related to the refrain than to each other. The refrain recurs so frequently that it can occupy the major part of the sung performance.

Songs are performed in different ragas, 'musical modes'. In manuscripts and in printed editions the name of the raga is given before each song. Different manuscripts can give not only variant readings of the texts, they may also ascribe different ragas to the same song. For example, both *Āsāvarī* and *Rāmagiri* ragas are ascribed to the song 'The world is my guru . . .'

The songs attributed to Ānandghan use a variety of ragas. The northern Indian tradition of classical music assigns ragas for performance at certain parts of the day and often links them to particular Indian seasons. The various treatises on music, however, do not necessarily agree in their attributions.[46] The most frequently used raga in the songs of Ānandghan is the cold-season, midday, or morning, Āsāvarī raga, the mode of twenty to twenty-four of the poems. Other ragas ascribed

[46] The following attributions are taken from Vasanta 1970 pp. 14–20 and from Shukla 2001 pp. 17–20. These are modern attributions and may not reflect performance in the eighteenth century.

to the songs are the spring, early morning or night *Belāvala/ Bilāvala* (eight poems), the cold-season, afternoon or midday *Dhanyāśrī* (six), the cold-season, evening or afternoon *Gauḍī* (six, seven or eight), the hot-season, midday *Kānharā/Kānhaṛo* (five or six), the hot-season, midnight or midday *Kedārā* (four), the cold-season, late afternoon *Mārū* (five), the cold-season, noon *Ṭoḍī* (eight), the spring, late night or afternoon *Vasanta* (ten or eleven) as well as two night ragas, *Sāraṅga* (seven or eight) and *Soraṭha* (seven or eight). Nine songs in the *Granthāvalī* do not have any indication of raga.

Connections between the themes of the songs and their raga attribution are not always clear, yet we can observe some tendencies in our collections. It is intriguing to note the absence of ragas linked to the rainy season—this was the time when Jain ascetics stayed in one place and, consequently, had more interaction with people than during their wanderings in the other seasons of the year.

As noted above, the raga most frequently employed in the songs is Āsāvarī, a plaintive mode said to originate in a snake-charmer's melody. Although the concept of ragas originated in Indian music, a theme of painting developed which attempted to evoke aspects of the ragas by visual means, and the Āsāvarī raga, or rather *rāgiṇī* in its feminine aspect, was frequently depicted in miniature paintings as a dark-skinned tribal girl, garlanded with snakes and wearing a skirt of leaves. She sits alone in a mountain forest near a brook and in the absence of her lover she talks to a cobra held in her hand. Ānandghan's songs in the Āsāvarī raga generally address an ascetic, *avadhū*, and speak about true wisdom contrasted with the workings of māyā. Ānandghan used the Āsāvarī, which is classified as an early morning or occasionally a midday or night raga, to express regret for lost time and as an exhortation to wake up to a life spent in search of the transcendental. The first songs in the *Bahattarī*, like the *Belāvala* raga, are also in a morning mode, and likewise, they contain transcendental exhortations. Early morning songs urging people to wake up to a transcendental life have a function similar to that of the Vedic *Gāyatrī* prayer recited by many orthoprax Brahmins in the morning so as to facilitate the divine awakening of the mind and soul. Early morning songs have been common in India since at least the early modern times. For example, *prabhātiyuṁ*, the daybreak song is one of the most popular genres attributed to the most famous fifteenth-century Gujarati Vaishnava poet, Narsī Mehtā.

Ānandghan's songs in the Sāraṅga raga tend to praise the inner experience, anubhava, while many in the Ṭoḍī raga present, the words of a woman with wounded pride, the khaṇḍitā. Those of the Vasanta or Kānhaṛo ragas tend to describe the pangs of separation. Songs in these ragas are often related to the spring festival of Holi and normally express the words of a heroine who on seeing the festivities is dejected because her lover is absent.

The bonfire of the Holi festival is lit with songs one night in spring.
My mind is burning every day and the ashes of my body are scattered by the wind. Without my lover I forgot good sense.

A peculiarity of the songs is the proliferation of addresses to the audience, such as 'truthful brother', or 'ascetic' etc. and also of many adversative exclamations, which we have translated as 'Oh', 'Hey', 'You see', 'Look', 'Bah', etc. In performance, these addresses and exclamations would have heightened the directness of the auditor's emotional response. A similar response would have been felt when the poems were recited without musical accompaniment. Even when read on one's own, these interjections would have had a similar effect, since it was usual to read aloud, as remains the practice among many people in India today when reading material of a traditional nature.

Written Transmission

Soon after their composition, some of the songs were put into written form either by being placed in short sequences of some three to fifteen songs or by being incorporated into collections of similar poems by various authors. Medium-sized Ānandghan anthologies, each containing some forty to sixty songs, emerged between 1699 and 1741. By 1775, the date of the first longer surviving manuscript,[47] some scribe with the aim of collecting all songs of the great poet had formed the collection known as the *Bahattarī* (Collection of Seventy-two). This collection determined the subsequent course of transmission until the appearance of printed books, such as Jñānsundar's *Ānandghan Pad Muktāvalī* and Bhimsingh Manak's *Ānandghan Pad Muktāvalī*[48] and Bhimsingh Manak's *Ānandghan Bahattarī*, a collection of 107 pads that appeared in his book *Prakaraṇ Ratnākar* in 1876.

The variant readings in most of the Bahattarī manuscripts suggest that they all stem from a common written archetype. Most of the variants are orthographic or contain omissions of one or two syllables, often making the word incomprehensible, and are indicative of written transmission, as is the absence of *geyavikāras*, which are variations typical of oral transmission, such as the inversion of lines, adjustments to the rhythm, the

[47] Manuscript called *Adhhyātma Gīt* (Transcendental Songs) in Oriental Institute, Vadodara, No. 16457.

[48] This book is cited in Kharaid p. 3 and Nahta p. 37. I was not able to consult a copy of it.

use of fillers, variations in the beat or modifications of the refrain.[49] Most Bahattarī manuscripts present more or less the same song sequence with only occasional differences. This collection can be considered as the eighteenth- and nineteenth-century literary canon of Ānandghan's songs.

The number of songs in the Bahattarī manuscripts varies between seventy-five and eighty-nine since new songs continued to be appended to the original collection of seventy-five songs. This number increased still further in 1876 when Bhimsingh Manak published, within the first volume of his *Prakaraṇ Ratnākar*, his edition of 107 songs collected from several manuscripts. Manak's sequence has been incorporated into many subsequent editions including the well-known Bombay edition (1955–63) of Motichand Girdharlal Kaparia, which also gives some variant readings and a comprehensive Gujarati commentary on the spiritual meaning of each pad. In the little-known *Ānandghan Granthāvalī*—which is a critical edition based on four manuscripts and on three earlier editions—Umravchand Jargad has 124 collected songs. Today we know of 152 songs that have been attributed to Ānandghan in one way or another.

As far as the oldest collections are concerned, one can conjecture that they were not ad hoc compilations of whatever was available but were formed on a thematic basis. Shared sequences based on ragas can be observed at various points throughout the collections, suggesting that they may have been the original 'bricks' from which these old, medium-sized collections were built. A close analysis of the contents of manuscripts B and A, as given in the concordance of the *Granthāvalī*, leads to the conclusion that the number of songs

[49] A study of *geyavikāra*s can be found in Callewaert and Lath 1989 pp. 63–82.

using love imagery tends to be higher in manuscript A, whereas there is a greater number of poems with hortatory and philosophical content in manuscript B. Furthermore, there are ten songs that are not present in the shortest and earliest Bahattarī collections but are attested in one or more early manuscripts.[50] Two of these songs—'My life is the Cloud of Bliss . . .' (38) and 'Mother, no one at all has left me impartial!' (39)—although not found in the earliest Bahattarīs of seventy-five songs, were incorporated into some of the later Bahattarī manuscripts.[51]

The ten early songs that are not found in the early Bahattarīs do not appear to have been omitted on the basis of any theological divergence from the songs that were included. The only exception seems to be the relatively long song with the refrain 'My friend, no one at all left me impartial!' (39). It may have been excluded on the grounds that it seems to be explicitly opposed to any theological system, including that of the Jains. One excluded song[52] shows a stronger Gujarati influence in its language than most of those in the *Bahattarī* collection. However, other songs with strong Gujarati features—like 'Hey, someone stop the habit . . .' (25) and 'The amount is small . . .' (36)—are included in the canon. This indicates that Gujarati features did not seem to have been firm grounds for rejection. With regards to the remaining eight poems rejected from the early Bahattarīs, the modern editor Jargad considered most of them to be inauthentic on stylistic grounds. Their style and imagery certainly tend to be simpler than that of the other songs; however, there are reasons that relate to their form that could have led to their exclusion. Five of them appear in manuscript O.

[50] 66, 72, 70, 78, 79, 80, 83, 88, 105 and 118 in the *Granthāvalī*.

[51] 66 and 72 in the *Granthāvalī*.

[52] 88 in the *Granthāvalī*, not included in our volume.

They are in the Vasanta raga in a metre close to that of the most popular metrical form used in early Jain narratives, the *caupāī*.[53] They are without a metrically distinctive refrain. Hence, their specific metre and raga must have been the reason these songs were excluded from the canonical collection, since it contains no other songs in that metre or raga. The refrain has particular importance in communal singing, since that is the part of the song in which the audience can join; consequently a song without a refrain is less suited to communal performance. The strength of a conscious rejection is indicated by the fact that even an initially popular song attested in three out of the four old manuscripts[54] has also been omitted from the canon.

The nature of the initial oral and later written transmission makes it likely that our received text is not necessarily the text composed by Ānandghan. It is also due to the flaws of oral transmission that some of Ānandghan's songs are often incorrectly attributed to other poets like Kabīr,[55] Sūrdās, Banārsīdās[56] or Dyānatrāy.[57] Since most of these songs are not present in the old manuscripts we have a sound reason to discard them. Nevertheless, they already had a quality that allowed for them to be absorbed into the Ānandghan-corpus, after which they have also been slightly reworked. We have, therefore, included one such poem, 'Give up, mind, the company of crooked Bad Understanding' (*Taja mana kumatā kuṭila ko saṅga*),

53 Each line in them has two rhyming half-lines of sixteen mora. The half-lines end in long-short metrical sequences as in the fifteen-mora caupāī, and not two long syllables as in the sixteen-mora caupāī.

54 The song *'Kita jāṇa matai ho prāṇanātha . . .'* (*Granthāvalī* 80), not included in our volume, is present in manuscripts O, A, C.

55 Nahta, Agarchand 1978; Nahta, Agarchand 1974 pp. 35–36; Kharaid p. 226.

56 Kharaid pp. 227, 229.

57 Jain p. 208; Shukla p. 132. See also Kharaid pp. 4–5 and p. 224.

also attributed to Sūrdās, into our translation. This famous song travelled from one collection to another. It was attributed to Sūrdās in manuscript tradition as early as 1638.[58] Moreover, this pad with a variant in its refrain, 'Give up, mind, the company of those confused about Hari' (*Chāṁḍi mana hari bimuḍḍhana kau saṅga*)—but still attributed to Sūrdās—is present in several seventeenth- and eighteenth-century manuscripts of the *Guru Granth Sāhib*, the sacred book of the Sikhs. The modern editions, however, give only its title line. This line already appeared in the Kartarpur Pothi of 1604 showing that the poem was in circulation by the end of the sixteenth century.[59] The first line must have reminded some scribes of the imagery of Ānandghan's kumati songs. This song with the signature of Sūrdās was included into a composite manuscript containing mostly Ānandghan's songs,[60] which may have facilitated the shift of authorship in later transmission. Since this song is not present in any early Ānandghan manuscript one can suspect that someone reworked the beginning and the signature in what he thought to be Ānandghan's spirit.

There are, however, a number of songs that are not present in the 'Collections of Seventy-two' and not attributed to other poets that may or may not be authentic. To illustrate this extra-canonical tradition we have included five songs not present in any of Jargad's manuscripts but only in published books. Later, at the time of the edition of the *Ānandghan Granthāvalī* the editor found a relatively early manuscript in which two of these songs were present.[61]

[58] Bryant and Hawley (forthcoming) No. 414 and Deol 2000 p. 185 note 80.
[59] Mann 2001 pp. 116–117, 175. Deol 2000 pp. 184–190.
[60] Shri Abhaya Jain Granthalay, Bikaner, Ms. 8033 f. 1r. The first six folios of this undated manuscript contain thirty-six songs of Ānandghan and nineteen others of Samaysundar, Jinrāj, Bhadrasen and other poets.
[61] Kharaid p. 15, note 3.

The Text of the Present Edition

The Sequence of Songs

The pads are placed into three groups: the hortatory and philosophical songs comprise the 'Songs of Wisdom' (1–15); the songs in which love imagery is dominant form part of the 'Songs of Love' (16–36); and the seventeen miscellaneous songs that did not appear in the early Bahattarī collections are called 'Songs Forgotten' (37–53).

The sequence of songs in our first two groups follow the sequence of the two early collections, B and A respectively, and consequently also follow the sequence of songs in the 'Collection of Seventy-two', which is based on these compilations. The third group follows the sequence of the *Sphuṭ Pad* (Miscellaneous Songs) given in the *Ānandghan Granthāvalī*, with the addition of two final songs—one from a printed edition (52) and one from a manuscript (53). Our first group, 'Songs of Wisdom', which is based on manuscript B, contains pads in the Belāvala, Dhanyāśrī, Ṭoḍī, Āsāvarī and Sāraṅga ragas. Our second group, 'Songs of Love', corresponding to the second part of the *Bahattarī*, contains twenty-one songs in twelve different ragas, most of them being originally part of collection A, in which the dominant theme is love.

The English Translation

Our translation is literary rather than informational; in other words, our aim is to provide the reader with an appreciative understanding of Ānandghan's songs by means of the translation itself; brackets, notes and other paraphernalia have been kept to a minimum. Ānandghan's voice is direct and, in places, abrupt; our use of language is intended to reflect this. Ānandghan is fond of puns or plays on words, and we have translated words with double meaning (*śleṣas*) in a resolved form: for example, the word *pāgharī* meaning both 'turban' and 'quarter of an hour' is translated as the 'turban of a quarter-hour' and a note indicates the presence of a pun in the original text.

In previous printed editions, and also in manuscripts, the refrain is not usually written in full after each verse unit but is instead indicated by its opening words only. In performance the refrain is sung as many times as the performers feel appropriate. Our text is closer to a sung version inasmuch as the refrain is given in full but only once after each verse unit.

There are places where we have been unable to interpret the original text with certainty and in such instances previous commentators on the text are usually of little help. It may be that the original text has been corrupted or that Ānandghan's thought has proved too elusive for subsequent readers. In such cases we have given what we think is the most likely interpretation and indicated the uncertainty in the notes.

There can be no definitive translation of any literary work. Our translation of Ānandghan's songs is determined by our time and place. We are aware that our understanding of South Asian cultures is imperfect and that our standpoint within a Western cultural environment is both a strength and a weakness. Nevertheless, despite our limitations, we hope we have enabled readers of English to appreciate a great poet, whose works transcend the limitations of his own time and place.

Transcendental Songs of Ānandghan

Songs of Wisdom

1

Raga Belāvala

Hey, you dullard, why are you asleep? Get up, awake!

Life is slipping away like water from folded hands;
look, the watchman is striking the hour.
Hey, you dullard, why are you asleep? Get up, awake!

Indra, the Moon, the lords of the Nāgas and the lords of the sages passed away. Oh, what is a king, a sultan or a prince?
Wandering and wandering in the ocean of existence you have received, in your nature, the boat of devotion to the Lord.
Hey, you dullard, why are you asleep? Get up, awake!

Why do you delay, you dimwit? Cross and reach the far shore of the waters of existence!
Meditate on the Cloud of Bliss, the form full of consciousness, the pure, untainted god.
Hey, you dullard, why are you asleep? Get up, awake!

2

Raga Belāvala

Hey, you dull-witted watchman, do not strike the hours!

Men have bound turbans of quarter-hours around their heads—
 why do you tell the hours?
Hey, you dull-witted watchman, do not strike the hours!

You know only the art of the particles of time and death but
 you do not gain the Undivided, the Timeless.
The clock that measures the play of the Timeless is forged within
 the pot of the body—that is the clock that pleases me.
Hey, you dull-witted watchman, do not strike the hours!

It is full of the essence of the experience of the self, no other
 thing can be contained in it.
Only the exceptional obtain this never-changing art of the
 Cloud of Bliss.
Hey, you dull-witted watchman, do not strike the hours!

3

Raga Belāvala

The soul thinks its hour successful.

Intoxicated with children, wife, wealth and youth it has forgotten the suffering in the womb.
The soul thinks its hour successful.

Completely heedless, it does not regard anything; it grasps stubbornness like a green pigeon does a stick.
When death, the black bombardier, suddenly arrives, he will grab you like a lion does a goat.
The soul thinks its hour successful.

It is attached to a dream kingdom imagined real; it is excited about the shadow of a cloud on the sky.
Abandoning the diamond, the Cloud of Bliss, people are infatuated with the pebble of illusion.
The soul thinks its hour successful.

4

Raga Dhanyāśrī

Foolishness is a hunchbacked woman of crooked ways,
Intelligence is like Rādhā.
When they are playing the chess of four ways, Rādhā wins, the
hunchback loses.

My soul plays the chess of four ways.

Who cares for draughts or cards? The intelligent pay no account
to them.
My soul plays the chess of four ways.

You yourself have prepared with affection the dice of passion,
sin and illusion.
As the cast of the dice falls, so moves the piece when it's played.
My soul plays the chess of four ways.

Under the five is the two, my friend; the one is under the six.
Adding all together the amount is equal; this is the science of
calculation.
My soul plays the chess of four ways.

The green one roams among the eighty-four; the black does
not break away.
The red and the yellow return home; sometimes the partners
break up.
My soul plays the chess of four ways.

Until the ace of the partner Discernment comes, the game is
unfinished.
When the lord, the Cloud of Bliss, shows an ace, then does the
soul triumphantly win.
My soul plays the chess of four ways.

5

Raga Ṭoḍī

Look at me, I'm pining away day and night without my lover!

I've done with respect for great and small; I never turn my eyes
from the door.
Look at me, I'm pining away day and night without my lover!

Clothes and jewellery ignite my body. Look, no inlaid pendant
pleases me.
Shiva and Lakshmi bring no happiness, my friend; what's an
immortal goddess worth?
Look at me, I'm pining away day and night without my lover!

My mother-in-law's trust does not last for a sigh; look, my
deformed sister-in-law fights from daybreak.
No other doctor soothes the heat; the Cloud of Bliss showers
nectar.
Look at me, I'm pining away day and night without my lover!

6

Raga Ṭoḍī

Beguiling woman, get away! You, embrace me and wake up!

An illusion, Egoism, sports with you—she, the cheater of my heart and of Experience.
Beguiling woman, get away! You, embrace me and wake up!

Brother, mother, father, relative, clan—don't strike me as brilliant.
Every day I'm immersed in drinking the nectar of his taste, sight, touch and sound.
Beguiling woman, get away! You, embrace me and wake up!

The pain of one bereft of the lord of her life—I can't get to the far shore of it; my feet are tired.
It's difficult to attain the sight of the Cloud of Bliss. I'm looking for a boat to cross over to the bank.
Beguiling woman, get away! You, embrace me and wake up!

7

Raga Ṭoḍī

I'm yours! I'm yours! That's what I keep saying.

If you deny these words, I'll go to Benares and undergo the saw.
I'm yours! I'm yours! That's what I keep saying.

I find nothing in the Vedas, the Legends, the Book, the Quran, the Doctrine and the Scripture, you see.
The spring song has burst out and taught everything well; I abide tinted in your colour and essence.
I'm yours! I'm yours! That's what I keep saying.

I just want you to be pleased; a million times I put up with the gossip of others.
Lord Cloud of Bliss, come fast, beloved, otherwise I'll flow in the waves of the Ganges.
I'm yours! I'm yours! That's what I keep saying.

8

Raga Āsāvarī

The course of the chain of hope in the world goes upside down, absolutely topsy-turvy.
The one in chains runs around in the world; the freed one stays in the same place.

Ascetic, why are you sleeping in the body's monastery? Wake up, look in the vessel!

Don't trust the monastery of the body, it collapses in a twinkling. Still the stirring, attend the vessel; can there be a reflection in frolicking water?
Ascetic, why are you sleeping in the body's temple? Wake up, look in the vessel!

In the monastery there is a lodging for five spooks; in the breath, a cunning headless demon.
Every second they are trying to cheat you—don't you understand, you blockhead?
Ascetic, why are you sleeping in the body's temple? Wake up, look in the vessel!

The supreme being is different from the visible world; in the pot of the body the window is subtle.
With the practice of the self, the exceptional shines and glimpses the pole star.
Ascetic, why are you sleeping in the body's temple? Wake up, look in the vessel!

Killing hope he takes a posture in the pot of the body and rouses the wordless prayer.
He receives the stainless Lord, the form of consciousness, the Cloud of Bliss.
Ascetic, why are you sleeping in the body's temple? Wake up, look in the vessel!

9

Raga Āsāvarī

Ascetics! What shall I, lacking good qualities, demand? For he is expert, his qualities are like the sky.

I don't know singing; I don't know music; I don't know how to distinguish the notes, bah!
I don't know how to be pleased; I don't know how to please; I don't know lowly attendance.
Ascetics! What shall I, lacking good qualities, demand? For he is expert, his qualities are like the sky.

I don't know the Veda, I don't know the Book; I don't know the types of metre.
I don't know logic and reasoning; I don't know the knacks of the poets.
Ascetics! What shall I, lacking good qualities, demand? For he is expert, his qualities are like the sky.

I don't know murmured prayers, I don't know responses; I don't know the expounding of stories, bah!
I don't know the sentiments, I don't know devotion; I don't know cold and hot.
Ascetics! What shall I, lacking good qualities, demand? For he is expert, his qualities are like the sky.

I don't know knowledge, I don't know science; I don't know the art of hymning.
I keep repeating 'Abode of good qualities' at the door of the house of my lord, the Cloud of Bliss.
Ascetics! What shall I, lacking good qualities, demand? For he is expert, his qualities are like the sky.

10

Raga Āsāvarī

Ascetic, it's a city-showman's show! Priests and judges don't understand.

One time it remains fixed; at that very time it appears and vanishes.
A steady being changing up and down!—I've never heard of this before.
Ascetic, it's a city-showman's show! Priests and judges don't understand.

One is many and many one again, as an earring is just gold in its nature.
As billows in water, pots in earth, rays in sun, countless things are held in it.
Ascetic, it's a city-showman's show! Priests and judges don't understand.

Is, is not, not in words, unreachable to senses; is this evidenced by the standpoints, and the sevenfold?
Some exceptional unprejudiced one recognizes it—how could opinion-warriors see?
Ascetic, it's a city-showman's show! Priests and judges don't understand.

The one, who considers it all-pervading, all-embodying, delighting in its independent existence, through the nectar of the speech of the Cloud of Bliss, can attain the supreme aim.
Ascetic, it's a city-showman's show! Priests and judges don't understand.

11

Raga Āsāvarī

Ascetic! The one who preserves my name savours the supreme essence.

I am not man, I am not woman; I have no rank, no class. No caste, no lineage, not a holy man, not a disciple, I am not light nor heavy.
Ascetic! The one who preserves my name savours the supreme essence.

I am not hot, I am not cold; I am not long nor short. I am not brother, I am not sister; I am not father nor son.
Ascetic! The one who preserves my name savours the supreme essence.

I am not mind, I am not speech; I am not the ground of the body.
I am not the guise, I am not the wearer of the guise; I am not the doer nor the deed.
Ascetic! The one who preserves my name savours the supreme essence.

I am not sight, I am not touch; I am not taste nor smell at all.
The servants sacrifice themselves for the image of consciousness, the Cloud of Bliss.
Ascetic! The one who preserves my name savours the supreme essence.

12

Raga Āsāvarī

Truthful brother, wander with Equanimity. Ascetic, do not be tainted by Attachment.

No, there is no wealth in affection; as you wander around your selfishness is wrapped up.
You will abandon couches, thrones and millions of palanquins; at the end you will be laid in the dust.
Truthful brother, wander with Equanimity. Ascetic, do not be tainted by Attachment.

The madman buries his wealth in the earth; he brings dirt onto his own head.
It will become the den of rats and snakes; therefore it is named inauspicious.
Truthful brother, wander with Equanimity. Ascetic, do not be tainted by Attachment.

Equanimity is the daughter of the jewel-giving ocean, her brother the moon of Experience.
Leave the deadly poison in the cup of worldly existence; yourself take the nectar.
Truthful brother, wander with Equanimity. Ascetic, do not be tainted by Attachment.

Those beings with thousands of eyes and feet and with four heads are extremely frightened of them.
The Supreme Being, the cloud-of-bliss lover embraces her with benevolence.
Truthful brother, wander with Equanimity. Ascetic, do not be tainted by Attachment.

13

Raga Sāraṅga

The flower of Experience of the self has a novel way.
The nose does not grasp its fancy; the ear gets the experience.

Experience, why don't you arouse the Lord?

Purity along with attachment is like milking a wart on a goat's neck.
Experience, why don't you arouse the Lord?

Don't you be vexed by what I say; you're the one who taught this.
Saying it over again is like showing a finger to a snake.
Experience, why don't you arouse the Lord?

Consciousness is steeped in the colours of others; it itself speaks intoxication.
Equanimity belongs to the Cloud of Bliss; can't *that* be called cloud of bliss?
Experience, why don't you arouse the Lord?

14

Raga Sāraṅga

Experience, you are my good friend.

Come, think of a clever strategy; prevent the attachment of the other.
Experience, you are my good friend.

Thirst, a whore, the daughter of a jester, how can she keep the house straight?
She feeds her family of rogues, swindlers and tricksters; why not keep it in mind?
Experience, you are my good friend.

Why lose reputation sporting with a crafty, malevolent bawd?
When Equanimity, the Cloud of Bliss, comes home, then the drums of victory will sound.
Experience, you are my good friend.

15

Raga Sāraṅga

Experience, after all I am your loyal servant.
I don't know where this illusion, Egoism, comes from; I don't know where she lives.
Experience, after all I am your loyal servant.

The Mind delights with her. Why are you cast down?
She never stops bothering the beloved. The whole world laughs.
Experience, after all I am your loyal servant.

My cruel husband doesn't understand a thing; a single moment passes like six months.
The home of the lord, the Cloud of Bliss, is Equanimity—the other is conjecture and disguise.
Experience, after all I am your loyal servant.

Songs of Love

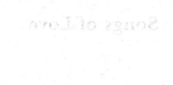

16

Raga Vasanta Dhamāra

The juice of the self's experience cannot be drunk from a cup of words.
The drunk collapses, the sober digests it.

You call my beautiful beloved a softy, my friend; why are you speaking hot words?

No bumpkin talks about his uncle in front of his mother. 'It's a pack of lies!' What are you talking about, my good woman?
You call my beautiful beloved a softy; my friend, why are you speaking hot words?

'He won't abandon the palace of the four ways. How could my lord come?'
No eating, no drinking in this state; your laughing breaks my bones.
You call my beautiful beloved a softy; my friend, why are you speaking hot words?

'He is having fun in Attachment's bed, dozing day and night.'
There's no give and take in these words; he comes and goes at dawn.
You call my beautiful beloved a softy; my friend, why are you speaking hot words?

'Listen, my lady,' says Faith, 'don't be so sad.
As you wait and wait your lord will come; the cloud of bliss will increase.'
You call my beautiful beloved a softy; my friend, why are you speaking hot words?

17

Raga Vasanta Dhamāra

The monsoon night passes like a knife—again and again the
heart is cut away.

Watching the beauty of my lover's picture I exclaimed 'beloved,
beloved, beloved, beloved!'
A cuckoo, skilled in taking life, echoes the same words.
The monsoon night passes like a knife—again and again the
heart is cut away.

One night because of the name of my beloved I completely
lost my senses.
The clever cuckoo kept giving reminder—'beloved, beloved,
beloved, beloved!'
The monsoon night passes like a knife—again and again the
heart is cut away.

Once I began to sing in the *Adana* raga.
Then the clever cuckoo takes up the note and provides a
rhythm—'beloved, beloved!'
The monsoon night passes like a knife—again and again the
heart is cut away.

As soon as the feelingless night has vanished, the sun of the
good nature rises.
As if the Cloud of Bliss would come and truly meet the good
consciousness of equanimity.
The monsoon night passes like a knife—again and again the
heart is cut away.

18

Raga Gauḍī Jakaḍī

The signs of the zodiac, moon, stars and ascendants—astrologer,
look this up in your almanac:
'When will the rover meet Equanimity, and the drought of
separation pass away?'

Without my beloved, alas, who will erase the terrible pain of
separation?

Seeing me in sorrow, sleep fled from my closed eyes.
My head goes on swaying like a lamp, my dear! My body does
not keep still for a winking of the eye.
Without my beloved, who will erase the lasting pain of
separation?

The cool moon and stars twinkle; lightning shines like a
sword.
The night intends to deceive me—even without my lover, Love
overwhelms.
Without my beloved, who will erase the lasting pain of
separation?

Fallen into the body's cage, my soul, the wild goose, is pining
away—it is not able to fly out.
The flame of the fire of separation is burning, my dear,—my
wings are lost from the roots.
Without my beloved, who will erase the lasting pain of
separation?

The night, a bawd, vainly contends with sighs deepening.
Dissuaded, sighs do not obey, my dear; stirred up, the night does not retreat. Without my beloved, who will erase the lasting pain of separation?

When a woman's lord is like this, because of him she remains unhappy.
When the lord, the Cloud of Bliss, arrives, he will fulfil her hopes in every way.
Without my beloved, who will erase the lasting pain of separation?

19

Raga Gauḍī

Calm your angry wife yourself, then; don't bring in go-betweens.

The deal of love is unfathomable—does its assessor understand?
The one who gives and takes he is the one who cares, my dear; no one else is agent.
Calm your angry wife yourself, then; don't bring in go-betweens.

Go and have a couple of words about life, then. Remove the grudge in her mind! Quench the body's burning, my dear; choose the words of nectar.
Calm your angry wife yourself, then; don't bring in go-betweens.

Give a little scawl, then don't make excuses, my lord.
Give a respectful greeting with a little look—attended with unchanging, immortal happiness.
Calm your angry wife yourself, then; don't bring in go-betweens.

The night is dark, the clouds are thick, I can't find the secret of the way.
By your grace I will make it; I will see the moon of your face.
Calm your angry wife yourself, then; don't bring in go-betweens.

Where there is love, there is no two ways, then; not the least authority.
The lord, the Cloud of Bliss came in person; he sat on the bed of Equanimity.
Calm your angry wife yourself, then; don't bring in go-betweens.

20

Raga Gauḍī

What sign shall I indicate, then? Through speech his form is not perceptible.

If I say 'one who has form', then it's nothing. How is a formless bound?
If I say 'one who has form and no form', my dear, thus the unequalled one is not perfect.
What sign shall I indicate, then? Through speech his form is not perceptible.

If I say 'the perfect one has form', then there is no consideration of bondage and liberation.
Being bound up in the cycle of existence, my dear, incarnation through sin and merit does not happen.
What sign shall I indicate, then? Through speech his form is not perceptible.

If I say 'he is perfect and eternal', then who comes into existence and passes away?
If I say 'the one who comes into existence and passes away', my dear, his ways are eternal and unbound.
What sign shall I indicate, then? Through speech his form is not perceptible.

The one with all the parts and the master of all the standpoints—all the proofs accept this.
The advocate of a standpoint clutches at straws, my dear, he makes place of fighting.
What sign of his shall I indicate, then? Through speech his form is not perceptible.

'A substance perceptible by inner experience'—that's the way to know him.
The great king, the Cloud of Bliss, my dear, isn't one to say or hear.
What sign shall I indicate, then? Through speech his form is not perceptible.

21

Raga Gauḍī

Now why is the theorist theorizing? Your discipline is unreachable, shoreless.

There is nothing holdable without a holding basis, you see; is there a basis without anything to hold? There is no egg without a chicken, my dear; does chicken exist without it? Now why is the theorist theorizing? Your discipline is unreachable, shoreless.

There is no bush without seed, you see; there is no seed without bush. No night happens without day, my dear; day without night is baseless. Now why is the theorist theorizing? Your discipline is unreachable, shoreless.

There is no perfect one without those involved in the world, you see; is there worldly involvement without the perfect ones? There is no act without an agent, my dear; is there agent without act? Now why is the theorist theorizing? Your discipline is unreachable, shoreless.

There is no birth without death, you see; no death without establishment in birth. There is no lamp without light, my dear; is there light without lamp? Now why is the theorist theorizing? Your discipline is unreachable, shoreless.

Grasp intently the fulfilment of the words of the lord, the Cloud of Bliss. Thinking of the eternal state of being, my dear; play without beginning, without end. Now why is the theorist theorizing? Your discipline is unreachable, shoreless.

22

Raga Kedāro

You simple people, I'm suffering; go ahead and laugh! How can I live at home without the beautiful Lord?

The pleasant bed, the moonlit night, the flower-garden and cool breeze—all my companions are flourishing with happiness; my mind's in fire, gone mad with this cursed separation.
You simple people, I'm suffering, go ahead and laugh! How can I live at home without the beautiful Lord?

Again and again I look at the earth and sky; your hiding, my beloved, is a spectacle for the people.
'Her body's skin and bone, her husband's not coming, he's left his dearest in hopelessness.'
You simple people, I'm suffering; go ahead and laugh! How can I live at home without the beautiful Lord?

Separation did whatever it liked with me. My life's in shame, if I don't get any news.
I will give an offering, if somebody says 'your beloved, the Cloud of Bliss is coming!' I'll light up the house.
You simple people, I'm suffering; go ahead and laugh! How can I live at home without the beautiful Lord?

23

Raga Mārū

Without my beloved my good sense is blocked.

At nighttime the snake of separation coils down on the bed.
Without my beloved my good sense is blocked.

Food, drink and words all gone; to whom can I speak straight?
The hope that he's coming today or tomorrow has vanished
from my mind.
Without my beloved my good sense is blocked.

The pain of separation is bottomless, its waters nine-spears deep.
What friend is a doctor to remove the ache from my heart?
Without my beloved my good sense is blocked.

Burying my face in my hands I sink into the river of plaintive songs.
Shedding tears I sprinkle the creeper of my hands.
Without my beloved my good sense is blocked.

Lightning flashes among thick clouds during the months of
the rains.
Rivers and lakes all are full; the pond of my body is dry.
Without my beloved my good sense is blocked.

Experience is speaking eloquently words that please:
'Equanimity, hold firm a while!—The Cloud of Bliss is coming.'
Without my beloved my good sense is blocked.

24

Raga Kānhaṛo

Without my lover I forgot good sense.

I swing with my eyes fixed on the window of the palace of grief.
Without my lover I forgot good sense.

I laughed seeing other women wasting away in body and mind.
But when I understood, I said only 'Nobody should fall in love!'
Without my lover I forgot good sense.

'How can I live without my lover, the dearest lord of my life?'
The snakes of separation drink up the breath of life.
Without my lover I forgot good sense.

Why apply cool fan, saffron or sandalwood paste?
This is not a fire but a fire of separation; they increase the burning
of the body.
Without my lover I forgot good sense.

The bonfire of the Holi festival is lit with songs one night in
spring.
My mind is burning every day and the ashes of my body are
scattered by the wind.
Without my lover I forgot good sense.

Come to my palace, Equanimity, and give the juice of your voice.
I'm at your service, lord, Cloud of Bliss. How can you be so cruel?
Without my lover I forgot good sense.

25

Raga Soraṭha

Hey, someone stop the habit of wandering to another man's house,
The young wife's habit of wandering to another man's house!

Going to other men's houses she became mendacious, she will bring a stain on her husband.
Hey, someone stop the habit of wandering to another man's house,
The young wife's habit of wandering to another man's house!

She's been seen crookedly coquetting and people will call her harlot.
Inducing the censure of everyone produces a thorn in the heart.
Hey, someone stop the habit of wandering to another man's house,
The young wife's habit of wandering to another man's house!

Good ladies, neighbours, look here a bit, she is being abused in vain!
When she delights in the colour of the Cloud of Bliss, then will her earrings flash on her fair face.
Hey, someone stop the habit of wandering to another man's house,
The young wife's habit of wandering to another man's house!

26

Raga Soraṭha

Won't someone help me meet my gold-coloured Lord?

The outline of collyrium does not please my eyes; let bathing burn in hell!
Won't someone help me meet my gold-coloured Lord?

What well-wisher would know the sufferings of another soul?—the separation is fathomless.
My body is shaking and runs around like a monkey.
Won't someone help me meet my gold-coloured Lord?

No body, no home, no affection, no beautiful form whatsoever; couplets and ballads don't please me.
I will hold my beloved lord, the Cloud of Bliss, in my arms, swelling with joy day and night.
Won't someone help me meet my gold-coloured Lord?

27

Raga Jaijaivantī

How did such a woman settle in the home? She is a worthless thing, you know.

In the house where she stays there will be disaster.
How did such a woman settle in the home? She is a worthless thing, you know.

Look, she'll cause utter disgrace when she enters the house.
Because this deceiving woman of the moment is the associate of the world, you know.
How did such a woman settle in the home? She is a worthless thing, you know.

She's not to be trusted with a cowrie; she'll eat up your elders, you know.
The Cloud of Bliss will listen; your maidservant humbly requests.
How did such a woman settle in the home? She is a worthless thing, you know.

28

Raga Jaijaivantī

My oath! My oath! My oath! I swear!

What do I keep from you? I'm telling you straight!
My oath! My oath! My oath! I swear!

Seeing you alienated my mind is penned in by sorrow;
The person you sport with—she is the servant of the world.
My oath! My oath! My oath! I swear!

You do not have anyone other than the one who would cut off
her head and put it in front of you.
I swear, Cloud of Bliss: I'm not telling you lies.
My oath! My oath! My oath! I swear!

29

Raga Āsāvarī

My lover is the one who looks sweet; the world looks sour.

A feast without my beloved is a cry of sorrow in the wilderness.
My lover is the one who looks sweet; the world looks sour.

There is enchantment in my lover; in the world distress.
Can gallons of milk and vinegar be stored in the same container?
My lover is the one who looks sweet; the world looks sour.

Without my lover is a fourfold destiny; to my mind it's hollow.
Collecting dues is swindling and fixing; money is the genuine cash.
My lover is the one who looks sweet; the world looks sour.

Without my lover my mind is a pipe from a well.
I bow to the Cloud of Bliss and drive away everything.
My lover is the one who looks sweet; the world looks sour.

30

Raga Āsāvarī

The world is my guru and I am the disciple of the world. The barrier of disputations has broken down.

The guru has all kinds of prosperity, power and wealth; there is a begging bowl and gloom in the disciple's house.
The world is my guru and I am the disciple of the world. The barrier of disputations has broken down.

Everything in the guru's house is studded with gems; the disciple's hut has only a thatched roof.
The world is my guru and I am the disciple of the world. The barrier of disputations has broken down.

The guru beats me with the stick of the word; the disciple's mind is thick with sins.
The world is my guru and I am the disciple of the world. The barrier of disputations has broken down.

One does not reach the depth of the guru's house; the Cloud of Bliss reveals the story of the unutterable.
The world is my guru and I am the disciple of the world. The barrier of disputations has broken down.

31

Raga Rāmagirī

My mind is set on the name of the Lord.

Public, private and intimate audiences—no use for legal hearings.
My mind is set on the name of the Lord.

Riches worth five, twenty-five, fifty thousand and millions.
They leave without eating, spending or giving. Their faces keep darkening.
My mind is set on the name of the Lord.

They belong neither here nor there, neither with God nor with this life; they remain entangled between two places.
Some truthful person says a clever thing: the Cloud of Bliss is the abode of excellences.
My mind is set on the name of the Lord.

32

Raga Dhanyāśrī

Experience, how will my lover be mindful?

Poor in one moment—wealthy in another; he puts on stained and stainless forms.
Experience, how will my lover be mindful?

He is the king of gods in a moment—then I see him as buttermilk; he is called unperishing.
He himself is the benefactor of separated people; he makes false accounts of his own wealth.
Experience, how will my lover be mindful?

You are my friend and I am your friend. Why do you then show difference?
Bring to me the lord, the Cloud of Bliss, otherwise play the music of farewell.
Experience, how will my lover be mindful?

33

Raga Dhanyāśrī

Now the untainted god is my lord and recourse.

Where shall I wander? Where shall I try to search? Where shall I delight people?
Now the untainted god is my lord and recourse.

I won't make up my eyes like the eyes of the wagtail; I don't need the collyrium of the mind's wealth.
My ornament, the Supreme Soul, is within my clay; he is the shatterer of all sins and the fears.
Now the untainted god is my lord and recourse.

This is my wish-granting cow, this is my horn of plenty, this is the bath in nectar.
The Cloud of Bliss is the lion of the forest of my body, the destruction for the mad elephant of desire.
Now the untainted god is my lord and recourse.

34
Raga Kāfi

The determination of my stubborn eyes doesn't pass away; they want to look again and again.
Looking at the picture of the beautiful boy they never have enough. Forced to turn away a bit, they, afflicted, weep.
The determination of my stubborn eyes doesn't pass away; they want to look again and again.

Like a crocodile they are fixed on the door of my beloved's beauty.
There is no constraint of shame in the mind; the shawl of family decency is thrown behind.
The determination of my stubborn eyes doesn't pass away; they want to look again and again.

Nothing imposes the slightest hindrance; they are not turned away a jot or a tittle.
The elephant stops at its own will; the mahaot has no strength.
The determination of my stubborn eyes doesn't pass away; they want to look again and again.

Listen, without my beloved Experience life's breath is leaving right away.
'Don't be dejected, clever woman—the Cloud of Bliss is not far.'
The determination of my stubborn eyes doesn't pass away; they want to look again and again.

35

Raga Āsāvarī

One may say Rama, Rahman, Krishna or Shiva, then.

One may say Lord Parshva, and say Brahma—all is the absolute itself.
One may say Rama, Rahman, Krishna or Shiva, then.

Various kinds of pots are named—they are the forms of the same clay.
One may say Rama, Rahman, Krishna or Shiva, then.

Thus, parts are imposed by imagination; his own form is undivided.
One may say Rama, Rahman, Krishna or Shiva, then.

36

Raga Prabhātī, Āsāvarī, Kalāharau

The amount is small, you see, brother, the interest high; how can it be paid back?

The whole principal amount is used up in interest, still it is not paid off.
The amount is small, you see, brother, the interest high; how can it be paid back?

Business has collapsed, you see, brother, by land and sea; you see, brother, they don't trust my credit.
If someone frees me by settling the instalments, I'll pay him the principal, I swear.
The amount is small, you see, brother, the interest high; how can it be paid back?

I will set up a fine shop in the main market; I will gain the respect of worthy people.
The lord, the Cloud of Bliss, is the crest-jewel of merchants; come and grasp my arm.
The amount is small, you see, brother, the interest high; how can it be paid back?

Songs Forgotten

37

Bee from another land, I can't stand it any more!

The bee delights in the ketaki flower; the bud of equanimity blooms.
Bee from another land, I can't stand it any more!

Without you there is no peace; pining and pining my life passes away.
Bee from another land, I can't stand it any more!

Cloud of Bliss lord, waiting to meet you the blossom of my face is withering.
Bee from another land, I can't stand it any more!

38

Raga Mārū Jaṅgalī

My friend, no one at all left me impartial! I longed so much
to be impartial; slowly they whispered their own opinions
into me.

A sorcerer met me and made me a sorceress; a monk made me
a nun;
A devotee grabbed me and made me a devotee; one intoxicated
with belief made me a believer.
My friend, no one at all left me impartial! I longed so much
to be impartial; slowly they whispered their own opinions
into me.

I studied Rama, they taught me Rahman, Jain worthies made
me recite.
I was attached to chores in house after house, unattached to
my life-relation.
My friend, no one at all left me impartial! I longed so much
to be impartial; slowly they whispered their own opinions
into me.

Someone shaved my head, someone plucked, someone wrapped
my hair.
Someone woke me up, someone left me sleeping—nobody
destroyed the pain.
My friend, no one at all left me impartial! I longed so much
to be impartial; slowly they whispered their own opinions
into me.

One established me, one uprooted me; one made me go, one made me stay.
I haven't seen anyone in agreement; no one is another's witness.
My friend, no one at all left me impartial! I longed so much to be impartial; slowly they whispered their own opinions into me.

The strong man pushes away the weak; cudgel strikes and strikes.
How can a frail woman talk in the kingdom of big warriors?
My friend, no one at all left me impartial! I longed so much to be impartial; slowly they whispered their own opinions into me.

Whatever I did, whatever I was made to do, I'm ashamed to tell.
Spoken in short, understand it in full; I have neither home, clothes nor ornaments.
My friend, no one at all left me impartial! I longed so much to be impartial; slowly they whispered their own opinions into me.

If I tell what I have gone through, he becomes angry; so I don't have the strength.
When the lord, the Cloud of Bliss holds my arm, the whole game goes right.
My friend, no one at all left me impartial! I longed so much to be impartial; slowly they whispered their own opinions into me.

39

Raga Jaijaivantī, Tritāla

My life is the Cloud of Bliss; my song the Cloud of Bliss.

My mother the Cloud of Bliss, my father the Cloud of Bliss.
My body the Cloud of Bliss, my offspring the Cloud of Bliss.
My life is the Cloud of Bliss; my song the Cloud of Bliss.

My king the Cloud of Bliss, my work the Cloud of Bliss.
My ornament the Cloud of Bliss, my modesty the Cloud of Bliss.
My life is the Cloud of Bliss; my song the Cloud of Bliss.

My sheen the Cloud of Bliss, my guts the Cloud of Bliss.
My centre the Cloud of Bliss, my growth the Cloud of Bliss.
My life is the Cloud of Bliss; my song the Cloud of Bliss.

40

Raga Vasanta

My dear life, know that this is true:
There, there isn't even as much prosperity as a grain.

There, don't be desirous; there isn't even any benefit.
Here, discrimination is standing, my dear, holding a staff.

There, a wicked thug of illusion, pride and fraud—
Here, your own family of honesty and tenderness.

There, anticipation, thirst, greed and anger.—
Here, peace, restraint and contentment shine.

There the arts of blackened sin pervade—
Here, plays the king himself, the Cloud of Bliss.

41

Raga Vasanta

Wake up, beloved, supreme master, supreme god: get rid of the gap between you and me!

My dear, wretched, vulgar modesty imposes on me all kinds of denials.
Wake up, beloved, supreme master, supreme god: get rid of the gap between you and me!

My dear, the baseless shawl of shame torments me. It puts an obstacle between you and me meeting.
Wake up, beloved, supreme master, supreme god: get rid of the gap between you and me!

My dear, my lord is intoxicated with another passion enjoying the company of the prostitute egoism.
Wake up, beloved, supreme master, supreme god: get rid of the gap between you and me!

Now, stupidity is knocked down from its roots. My mind blossoms in the spring of the Cloud of Bliss.
Wake up, beloved, supreme master, supreme god: get rid of the gap between you and me!

42

Raga Soraṭha Giranāṅ

Hey, why are you beating the boy, you child-murdering hag!

My boy is simple and innocent, speaks words of nectar.
Hey, why are you beating the boy, you child-murdering hag!

He has already started to toddle—have you gone blind?
You're sleeping at the head of your tomb; what son will give you bread?
Hey, why are you beating the boy, you child-murdering hag!

Concerning the five, the twenty-five and the fifty practices he speaks straight.
Lord, Cloud of Bliss, your servant! You are lord in every birth.
Hey, why are you beating the boy, you child-murdering hag!

43

Raga Soraṭha

You are my clever beloved who know my heart, my clever
heart-knowing beloved.

You did whatever I was thinking about. I recognize your
abundant love.
You are my clever beloved who know my heart, my clever
heart-knowing beloved.

You prepared a mansion of a drop of seed and filled it with light.
There are two thieves and two spies in it; nothing can be hidden.
You are my clever beloved who know my heart, my clever
heart-knowing beloved.

There are five and three women in the mansion, who govern
from this capital.
A woman subjugated the whole world—overcoming it with
the sword of knowledge!
You are my clever beloved who know my heart, my clever
heart-knowing beloved.

There are four men in the mansion—hungry, they are never
satiated.
One is of bad character, one genuine: the one who understands
it understands the wisdom of Brahma.
You are my clever beloved who know my heart, my clever
heart-knowing beloved.

You have spent seasons in the fourfold ways, but you did not recognize the working of karma.
The Cloud of Bliss understands this song; the righteous human being understood it.
You are my clever beloved who know my heart, my clever heart-knowing beloved.

44

Raga Aliyo Belāvala

Hey, mind, bring thought to the feet of the Jina! Sing the virtues of the Worthies!

Look, to fill her stomach the cow goes to the green.
Grazing the grass she goes all around but her mind is on her calf.
Hey, mind, bring thought to the feet of the Jina! Sing the virtues of the Worthies!

Look, five or six girls get together for water, clapping their hands and gurgling with laughter, but their mind is on their pot.
Hey, mind, bring thought to the feet of the Jina! Sing the virtues of the Worthies!

Look, the showman darts about in the marketplace, thousands of people make noises.
Grasping a cane he walks on the rope; his mind doesn't wander.
Hey, mind, bring thought to the feet of the Jina! Sing the virtues of the Worthies!

Look, gaming on the mind of the gamer; desire on the mind of the desirer.
The lord, the Cloud of Bliss, says: take the name of the lord like this.
Hey, mind, bring thought to the feet of the Jina! Sing the virtues of the Worthies!

45

Raga Belāvala

Bride, you're very stupid! Your lover's awake, you're asleep!

My lover's clever, I am just ignorant; I don't know what's going
to happen.
Bride, you're very stupid! Your lover's awake, you're asleep!

The Cloud of Bliss lover thirsts for your sight; lifting your veil
he will see your face.
Bride, you're very stupid! Your lover's awake, you're asleep!

46

Raga Mālasirī

With my child-husband my youth passes in vain.

These days are for laughing and playing; my friend, I pass the nights weeping.
With my child-husband my youth passes in vain.

Jewels and ornaments burn me; look, they don't suit my body at all.
A thought like this comes to mind: 'Let me take poison now!'
With my child-husband my youth passes in vain.

I don't sleep, I can't heave a sigh; I'm tormented within.
I'll become an ascetic, abandon home, and wander like the Cloud of Bliss.
With my child-husband my youth passes in vain.

47

Raga Āsāvarī

Look, my husband is a mere child; what shall I do with my youth?

My father was dull, the priest guilty and let lightning strike
the barber!
Look, my husband is a mere child; what shall I do with my youth?

They thought it was a good thing and betrothed us; where did
sin come from?
What to say of this house and family who've ruined my life?
Look, my husband is a mere child; what shall I do with my youth?

48

Raga Khamacha

Give up, mind, the company of crooked Bad Understanding;

From going with her stupidity is born and your acts of devotion
are destroyed.
Give up, mind, the company of crooked Bad Understanding.

Why give camphor to a crow to peck, bathe a dog in the Ganges,
smear a donkey with perfume, put ornaments on a monkey?
Give up, mind, the company of crooked Bad Understanding.

What happens if you feed it with milk? The snake will not give
up its venom.
The Cloud of Bliss says: the lord's dark blanket won't take on
any other colour.
Give up, mind, the company of crooked Bad Understanding.

49

Raga Lalita

Look, today there's a chance to meet Him!
Look, today there's a chance to meet Him!

Look, my sisters-in-law are bustling with work; His sister gave birth to a boy.
Look, today there's a chance to meet Him!

Look, my mother-in-law is preparing betel-leaves and sweetmeats; a curtain has been spread across.
Look, today there's a chance to meet Him!

Look, the auspicious arrival of my beloved, the Cloud of Bliss! Rapture is cloying in my heart.
Look, today there's a chance to meet Him!

50

Listen, spinning woman, your spinning wheel goes 'ay ay ay'.

Born in water, raised in land, settled in town—your self.
Hey, seen a wonder?—daughter gave birth to father.
Listen, spinning woman, your spinning wheel goes: ay ay ay.

You asked for the cotton of devotion; combed it with the comb of remembrance.
The carder of wisdom sat down to card. Look, the taut thread twangs.
Listen, spinning woman, your spinning wheel goes: ay ay ay.

A child, my marriage performed unawares. Look, the groom ignorant himself.
If she does not meet the ignorant groom, look, the girl gives birth to the father.
Listen, spinning woman, your spinning wheel goes: ay ay ay.

The mother-in-law is dead, the sister-in-law is dead, the husband and wife are dying.
Only an old woman isn't dying, look, to her the spinning wheel grants its speech.
Listen, spinning woman, your spinning wheel goes: ay ay ay.

My spinning wheel is resplendent with colours; look, the roll of cotton is in full bloom.
The spinning girl, a beauty, pulls up and counts the threads.
Listen, spinning woman, your spinning wheel goes: ay ay ay.

The one who wrote ‘ay ay’ on the spinning wheel—look, no one else writes ‘ay ay’.
If the Cloud of Bliss writes, then the coming and going has no power.
Listen, spinning woman, your spinning wheel goes: ay ay ay.

51

Raga Belāvala

How shall I meet my stainless friend?

Do I search far away among rivers and mountains, up in the clouds or deep in the ground?
How shall I meet my stainless friend?

I can't find him even by piercing the earth, and if I suffer fire, my body will burn.
How shall I meet my stainless friend?

The Cloud of Bliss says: 'O Jasa, listen to what I say: if I find this, then my wandering is averted!'
How shall I meet my stainless friend?

52

A deep cloud came pouring heavy rain.

In it hidden lightning flashes; darkness swells more and more.
A deep cloud came pouring heavy rain.

All around groups of clouds lower and time and again burst forth in thunder.
Torrential rain falls on the earth; even the tortoise has been defeated by its force.
A deep cloud came pouring heavy rain.

But he removed its fear; he led the waters of his existence into the ocean.
The Cloud of Bliss says, the lord of the victorious ones, Lord Parshva received the status of highest bliss.
A deep cloud came pouring heavy rain.

53

Raga Kedāro, Āśā Miśra

Five horses are harnessed to a wagon, their owner is sleeping inside.

The driver is a drunkard, the driver of the horses.
Five horses are harnessed to a wagon, their owner is sleeping inside.

The horses want to fly, the road is rough and they run in all directions.
Yet their dear master does not awaken, he who makes the horses gambol.
Five horses are harnessed to a wagon, their owner is sleeping inside.

The driver shouts 'Whoa!', the oblivious master feels annoyance.
The cart enters a jungle and gets entangled; its dozing master heeds nothing.
Five horses are harnessed to a wagon, their owner is sleeping inside.

Highwaymen and swindlers gather together, they foist alcohol on the two.
The cart is damaged in the jungle and its load is looted.
Five horses are harnessed to a wagon, their owner is sleeping inside.

When the master wakes up he sets the driver in his place; taking the bridle of life-breath he aims with an arrow.
He took the wagon in the forest to the road and reached the highest place of the 'Cloud of Bliss'.
Five horses are harnessed to a wagon, their owner is sleeping inside.

Notes to the Poems

Songs of Wisdom

1 *(Bahattarī 1; Granthāvalī 1)*

'lords of the Nāgas': *nāgendra*, 'Lord of the serpent-demons'. The commentators Motichand Kaparia and Umravchand Jargad identify it with *Dharaṇendra*, 'Lord of the Earth'. According to Jargad the words *indra candra naginda* refer to the lords of *indraloka, candraloka* and *nāgaloka*. It may be a loose reference to the three words.

'lords of the sages': Kaparia and Jargad interpret the word *muninda* 'great sage', 'best of sages' or its variant reading *muni* 'sage' as Tīrthaṅkara. The word *munīndra* was used in this sense already in Kundakunda's *Pravacanasāra*, a mystic work of the Digambar tradition said to date from the third century CE. Other popular Sanskrit works like the *Brahmapurāṇa* (110.34) or the *Bhāgavata Purāṇa* (10.67.27), however, used this word in the sense of 'best of sages'.

'you have received in your nature the boat of devotion to the Lord': The editions give several textual variants of this half line. The reading of the Bombay edition is '*bhramata bhramata bhava jaladhi pāyake bhagavanta bhajana binu bhāu nāū re*'. In his

Gujarati translation, however, Kaparia omits the interpretation of the word *pāyake*, 'having got', 'having received': 'Wandering and wandering in the ocean of existence, is there a boat of sentiments apart from the devotion to the Lord?'

2 *(Bahattarī 2; Granthāvalī 2)*

This poem is based on the popular Indian device of double meanings called *śleṣa* in classical aesthetics. In the translation śleṣas are given in a 'solved form'.

'turbans of quarter-hours': pun with the word *pāgharī*, which is a mixture of the words *pāv ghaṛī*—quarter-hour—and *pagṛī*—turban.

'art of the particles of': pun on the word *kalā*, 'art', 'particle'.

'time and death': pun on the word *kāla*, 'time', 'death'.

'Undivided, the Timeless': pun with the word *akal* which can be interpreted either as *a-kāl*, 'timeless', or *a-kalā*, 'without particles'.

'the clock that measures the play of the Timeless is forged': pun on the word *ghaṛī* 'clock, hour', 'is shaped, forged'.

'the pot of the body': pun on the double meaning of *ghaṭ*, 'pot' and 'body'.

'that is the clock': pun on the word ghaṛī meaning 'clock' and 'small pot' (*ghaṛā*). The imagery thus evoked with the puns is that of a pot. 'The particles of the Undivided are shaped into a pot and that is the pot that pleases me.'

'the essence': pun with the word *ras*, 'juice', 'essence' and thus continuing the imagery of the pot. 'It is full of the juice of the experience of the self.'

3 (*Bahattarī* 3; *Granthāvalī* 3)

'the suffering in the womb': According to the commentator Motichand Kaparia, the soul suffers from seclusion and the humiliation of an upside-down position.

'like a green pigeon does a stick': The green pigeon is said to keep a piece of wood in its beak. When this piece gets entangled, the bird omits a sorrowful cry but does not give it up.

4 *(Bahattarī 8; Granthāvalī 56)*

'hunchbacked woman': an allusion to a popular theme of Krishna poetry. After Krishna left the cowherd girls of Vrindaban, including his beloved Rādhā, he never returned to them. Once he healed a hunchback woman and enjoyed her company. It has become a recurring complaint of the cowherd girls that Krishna abandoned the beautiful Rādhā and passed his time with the hunchback.

'the chess of four ways': caupaṛa is a game played with an oblong dice on a cloth or board of cross-shaped layout, which is made of four strips or cloth with 96 squares. There are sixteen men of four colours: green, black, red, yellow and white and four rectangular dice with signs of 5, 6, 2, 1 in this order on each. Until a man hits another one, it is not allowed to go back to its original place. According to the commentators the word *caturagati/caturgati*, 'of four ways' apart from the four strips of the game, refers to the four types of life: hell-dwelling, plants-and-animals, human and divine. Jargad adds that the colours refer to the *leśyās*, 'conditions of the jīva' through which karma binds it.

'Under the five is the two, my friend; the one is under the six': The sum of any two diagonally opposite numerals on a dice is always seven. Numbers in Indian tradition are strongly associated with certain notions. Jargad and Kaparia interpret the number five as *pañcāśrava*, 'five engagements', Vishvanath Prasad Mishra as the five sense organs, while the number two is explained as passion and hatred and duality respectively. According to Jargad six means the six bodies and one the *asaṁyama pravṛitti* 'unrestrained behaviour', while to Mishra these numbers mean the six philosophies and the *brahman* respectively. One can also speak of the 'six enemies', *ṣadṛpu* (desire, anger, greed, delusion, intoxication, sins of the flesh—*kāma, krodha, lobha, moha, mada, māsalya*), and the one soul.

'the eighty-four': The concept of there being eighty-four lakh possible life forms into which a soul may be born is well-known to all Jains, as the details of the 84 lakh possibilities are recited as part of the *pratikramaṇa* ritual, in the vernacular recitation known generally as *sāt lākh*. See Cort 2002c, p. 75.

5 (*Bahattarī* 11; *Granthāvalī* 16)

6 (*Bahattarī* 13; *Granthāvalī* 17)

7 (*Bahattarī* 14; *Granthāvalī* 14)

'undergo the saw': The suicidal saw in Benares believed to grant heaven for those who die by it was a literary topos in the sixteenth and seventeenth centuries.

'spring song': Spring songs are, naturally, about love and longing. The word *cācarī* can also mean 'Yogic posture'.

'your colour': At the spring festival, coloured powder is thrown on the loved ones. Moreover, the word for colour, *raṅga* also means 'love'.

8 (*Bahattarī* 16; *Granthāvalī* 57)

'topsy-turvy': Jargad interprets the word mora as 'peacock' referring to a person who has eyes which do not see.

'blockhead': The interpretation is ambiguous. The word *sīsā* can also mean 'teaching'.

'different from the visible world': Jargad erroneously divides the first word into *nirapara paṁca* and translates as 'Having no other, the five supreme beings abide.'

'the window': Jargad explains that this window is *samyakatva*, a synonym for *samakit* and *samyak-darśana*, i.e., right faith or right worldview, one of the three gems of Jainism, as enunciated in the first verse of the Tattvārtha Sūtra.

9 *(Bahattarī* 19; *Granthāvalī* 10*)*

'sky': The Bombay edition and several manuscripts read *gaṇana*, 'count(ing)', instead of, *gagana*, 'sky': 'Those (who ask) are clever in counting their good qualities.'

'how to please': Jargad interprets this as 'to please God' and Kaparia as 'to fascinate someone'.

'lowly attendance': The *pada sevā*, 'the service of feet', literarily refers to the service of an image of a deity in a temple.

'the Book': Jargad interprets the Arabic loanword *kateb*, 'book' as *śāstra jñāna*, knowledge of traditional Indian books of science. In poem No. 14, however, it refers to the 'book of the Quran'.

'I keep repeating "Abode of good qualities"': Kaparia interprets this line as, 'I chant at the door of the Lord's house, the abode of excellences.'

10 *(Bahattarī* 20; *Granthāvalī* 59*)*

'Ascetic, it's a city-showman's show': Jargad interprets the showman as the Self (*ātman*) and the city as the body, while Kaparia claims that the ascetic is the Self and the juggler is 'consciousness' (cetan).

'the standpoints': The text here is emended on the basis of two of the most archaic *Bahattarī* manuscripts, d (Rajasthani Research Institute, Chopasni, No. 11634) and g (Oriental Institute Baroda, No. 16457) consulted from *nai* into *naya*, a word referring to the seven logical standpoints through which judgements can be made. (See Introduction.)

'the sevenfold': The commentators take this word as a reference to the seven elements of Jain logic.

'its independent existence': The text is uncertain here. Manuscript g reads an orthographic variant of our text (*sarabamāīṁ*), while the often more reliable manuscript d has *saraba naya*. The fourth line of 61 (*sarabaṅgī saba naya dhaṇī re, māne saba paravāna.*) also suggests the reading *saraba naya* meaning 'all the standpoints (consider it all-embodying)'. The commentaries do not agree in the interpretation of this line either. Our translation follows the explanation of Jargad stating that the self is all-pervading with regards to pure knowledge but transcendental with regards to the material world. This elucidation is made in the light of many-pointedness. Kaparia does not accept this as a reference to an all-pervading, all-embodying Self, and supposes two different subjects in the two halves of this line. 'Some (Vedāntins) consider it all-pervading, all-embodying, (but) the one who delights in its independent existence . . .'

11 *(Bahattarī* 22; *Granthāvalī* 11*)*

'a holy man': Several manuscripts give the reading *sādhana*, 'means'. With this word the sentence would be 'neither means, nor practicer'.

12 *(Bahattarī* 4; *Granthāvalī* 23*)*

'her brother the moon of Experience': An alternative interpretation is 'finds her delight in the moon of Experience'.

'Leave the deadly poison . . .': These two lines contain a reference to the churning of the milk ocean, when after a jewel, the moon and the deadly poison *kālakūṭa*, nectar, was at last gained by the gods.

'Those beings with thousands of eyes and feet and with four heads': According to Jargad this is a description of the demon of *moha*, 'delusion', with its four heads of anger, pride, illusion and greed. It can be a reference to the gods and demi-gods. Kaparia interprets it as a reference to the thousand-eyed Indra, the thousand-footed Śeṣanāga and to the four-headed Brahmā. Earlier Indian literature does not seem to corroborate the idea of the thousand-footed Śeṣa-snake. The term thousand-footed in the *Puruṣa-sūkta* (*Rigveda* 10.90.1.) refers to the Puruṣa himself (*sahasrapāt*) and in the *Vālmīki Rāmāyaṇa* (6.105.19) Brahmā addresses Rāma as *sahasracaraṇaḥ*. The overall meaning is unclear here. It probably means that the gods are afraid of Equanimity and of her brother, Experience. The commentators, however, stretching the syntax slightly, take the meaning as, 'There are beings with thousand eyes and feet and with four heads. She is very much afraid of them.' They agree that the pronoun 'she' refers to Equanimity.

13 *(Bahattarī 24; Granthāvalī 28)*

'the ear gets the experience': According to Jargad this is a reference to the *anāhata nāda*, the 'unbeaten sound' that a practitioner of yoga experiences when he or she reaches the divine within.

'Experience, why don't you arouse the Lord?': An alternative interpretation is 'Why don't you awaken the experience of the Lord?'

'can't *that* be called cloud of bliss?': Jargad interprets the pronoun 'that' as 'affection'.

14 *(Bahattarī 26; Granthāvalī 40)*

15 *(Bahattarī 27; Granthāvalī 43)*

'I am your loyal servant': It is an idiomatic expression to give strength to one's own words. Taking the word *rāvarī*, 'your', in its etymological sense 'belonging to the king', Kaparia interpreted this phrase as 'the King's maidservant'. According to the commentators apart from one line in the second strophe, 'Sumati', the chief wife, is complaining to her female companion, Experience, about how Māyā Mamatā—Illusion, Egotism—ensnared her husband, the Mind.

'I don't know where she lives': Claiming that somebody is of dubious origin is a way of abuse.

'The home of the lord, the Cloud of Bliss, is Equanimity': Mishra and Kaparia give a variant reading, *prabhu ghara kī samatā*—'Equanimity is of the home of the Lord'.

Songs of Love

16 *(Bahattarī 28; Granthāvalī 35)*

'The drunk collapses, the sober digests it': The words *matvālā*, intoxicated, and *nimatā*, sober, can also mean 'those who have doctrines' and 'disinterested' respectively. According to Kaparia, nimatā can even mean *syādvādmārgī* i.e. *anekāntavādī*.

The commentators say that the song following the couplet contains the words of personified Intelligence, Sumati, (Jargad) or Equanimity, Samatā, (Kaparia) to her friend

Faith, Śraddhā, about the Mind, Cetan, or Soul, Ātmārām, personified as her husband.

'softy': In his commentary Jargad implies that the word *narama*, soft, means *samarasī*, harmonious, equable, agreeable, inclined, willing.

'palace of the four ways': According to Jain doctrine the four embodiments for a soul are those of divine beings, human beings, animals and plants as well as hell-beings.

17 *(Bahattarī 32; Granthāvalī 34)*

'Raga Vasanta Dhamāra': Some manuscripts give the name of the raga as Vasanta, some as Dhamāra and one as Naṭamalāra.

'cuckoo': The Hindi word for 'beloved' is *piu*. The Indian cuckoo, which only sings from spring till the rainy season, is supposed to utter the same sound.

'echoes the same words': The text is ambiguous here. *Cavī*, interpreted as 'sound, words' is the reading of the *Granthāvalī*. The Bombay edition has the more straightforward *bīca*, 'in the middle, at the same time'. Some manuscripts read *vāci* or *vaci*, sound. Cavī may be a form of this word distorted by metathesis.

'completely': The Hindi has *nīu* '(from its) basis'.

'Adana raga': The interpretation of the word *aḍānai* is uncertain. Jargad takes it as a Marathi word meaning '(began to sing) at an inappropriate time' or 'at a distressful time'. Kaparia gives the less convincing 'without wisdom, prudence' interpretation probably relating it to the Gujarati *ḍahāpaṇ*, knowledge, or to the Persian *dān-* 'to know' with the negative prefix *a-*. *Aḍānā*, however, can also be the name of a musical mode.

'feelingless': The word *vibhāva* can also mean 'bright' or 'starry night'. It can also be interpreted as *vi-bhāva* 'being separated', 'separation' and thus referring to the night of separation.

'the sun of the good nature': The word *su-bhāva*, good nature or good sentiment is taken by Jargad as *sva-bhāva*, true nature, and thus referring to the sun of the true (i.e. divine) nature of the self.

18 *(Bahattarī 33; Granthāvalī 27)*

'almanac': The commentators agree that the word *jos* here is a corruption from *jyautiṣa* '(book) belonging to astrology' i.e. almanac although it is not attested in dictionaries.

'lightning shines': The meaning of the word *vinagī* is unclear. A close relation seems to be *vinagna*, naked (sword), although the commentators give meanings like 'not grasped' based probably on the less likely etymology of *vinā-graha*. The moon, the stars, the lightning, all these rekindle the longing for the beloved. Mishra interprets this line to be a sequel to the previous lines as the description of the face with unfolding metaphors: 'In the shelter of the face the eye is awake/twinkling with the lightning—sword of the separation—sparkling in it.'

'a woman's lord': *gṛhasvāmī*, '(house-)lord'.

'because of him she remains unhappy': Neither the subject of this line nor the reference of the pronoun *usasūṁ* 'with (because of) it/him/her' is clear. Apart from the interpretation translated earlier Kaparia mentions another possibility: The house is the 'house of impure nature' and its master is displeased with the soul (ātmārām). Jargad's interpretation is unclear: 'In this way, where is fortune in the fate of a woman whose master revels in impure behaviour? She is dejected because of the condition of her husband. (In spite of this she hopes) that the Cloud of Bliss . . . will fulfil her desires.'

'he will fulfil her hopes in every way': Mishra interprets the word *āya* as *āyu* 'age', 'life' creating the meaning 'my beloved will fulfil the hopes of my life'.

19 *(Bahattarī 34; Granthāvalī 36)*

'does its assessor understand?': Both Jargad and Kaparia cut the word *parikhana* 'the one who tests, inspects', into *parikha na* 'not (even) by inspecting it' and arrive at the meaning 'nobody understands it even by inspecting it'. The reading parikhana is given by Mishra.

'Go and have a couple of words about life, then': An alternative interpretation is 'Do (these) two things about your life!'

'Remove the grudge in her mind!': Jargad adds the negative syllable *na* to *meṭo*—'Why don't you remove the grudge from her (or your) mind?'

'Give a little scawl, then': The Hindi text is problematic. The word *kunajara* conceived by Jargad as the Persian *nazar*, sight or glance, prefixed with the Sanskritic *ku-*, bad, is probably a corruption. The Bombay edition and two of the manuscripts have the reading without the syllable *ku*. Their reading, however, seems to be simplistic: 'Look at her a bit with a glance.'

'I can't find the secret of the way': According to Jargad, it is now the woman (identified with Samatā, Equanimity) who speaks and thus these lines fit into the traditional image of *abhisārikā*, 'woman going out for a tryst'.

'the secret of the way': The word *phanda*, noose, trap can also mean 'secret'. Kaparia interprets this half line as 'Make it that I won't find obstacles on my way.'

20 *(Bahattarī 36; Granthāvalī 61)*

21 *(Bahattarī 37; Granthāvalī 62)*

22 *(Bahattarī 46; Granthāvalī 19)*

'are flourishing': Our reading *sātā*, good health or recovery, is based on two of the most archaic *Bahattarī* manuscripts, d (Rajasthani Research Institute, Chopasni, No. 11634) and g (Oriental Institute, Baroda, No. 16457), and coincides with the Bombay edition. For details of other manuscripts not collated in the *Granthāvalī* see Bangha 2008. The *Granthāvalī* has (*karai sukha*) *hāta*, 'acquire happiness'.

'hopelessness': Our reading *nirāsa* is based on manuscripts d and g and coincides with the Bombay edition and the variant of manuscript A in the *Granthāvalī*. The *Granthāvalī* has *nisāsā*, sigh.

23 *(Bahattarī 49; Granthāvalī 32)*

'the river of plaintive songs': The 'pain' meaning of the Braj word *sur* (S svara-), sound, cannot be attested in any dictionary although both commentaries interpret it in this sense. It was probably conceived as a form of the Braj word *sūla* (cf. Sanskrit *śūla*-), sharp pain. The compound *surasiṁdhu* referring to the rivers Ganges or Mandākinī can also be the name of a raga.

'words that please': Jargad interprets this as the words that please the beloved and persuade him to come, Kaparia takes them as 'the words that please Me'.

'Equanimity': Both commentators take the word samatā, equanimity, to be a vocative and identify 'Equanimity' with sumati the '(good) consciousness'.

24 *(Bahattarī* 50; *Granthāvalī* 26*)*

'I swing with my eyes fixed': The words *jhūlnā*, 'to swing', and *āṁkh lagānā*, 'to fix the eyes on', also can mean 'to be in suspense', 'to finish' and 'to fall in love with' respectively. A more abstract translation using these secondary meanings would be 'Fallen in love my eyes are wasted in (watching)'.

'Holi festival': A festival in the Indian month of Phalgun to celebrate the coming of the spring. A bonfire is lit on its eve.

'snakes of separation': The original reads 'snakes of the state of separation'. The image refers to the idea of the *pīvnā sāṁp*, a kind of snake that instead of biting with its poison sucks the life out of its victim.

'I'm at your service': Literally, 'I sacrifice myself (for you)'—an idiomatic expression to give strength to one's words.

25 *(Bahattarī* 52; *Granthāvalī* 47*)*

26 *(Bahattarī* 53; *Granthāvalī* 22*)*

'my gold-coloured Lord': It may be an echo of the iconography of some fordmakers such as Mahāvīra who are depicted as gold-coloured.

'let bathing burn in hell!': The Hindi idiomatic formula of swearing is 'May burning fall on the head of bathing!'

'beautiful form': The commentators interpret *reha na* as 'not the least (care for)' and take the meaning as 'I do not have the least (care for) body, home or affection.' The word reha (Sanskrit *rekhā*: 'line, contour'), however, can also mean 'form', hence 'beautiful form'.

27 *(Bahattarī 55; Granthāvalī 45)*

'She'll cause utter disgrace when she enters the house': Kaparia proposes a further, alternative interpretation for *sarama desī*, 'cause disgrace'. It can also mean '(be) the enemy (*dveṣī*) of grace'.

'this deceiving woman of the moment': The word *maisī* has been interpreted as *nimeṣī*, 'belonging to the moment'. Jargad takes it as a form of *meṣī*, she-goat, Mishra as a form of *mahiṣī*, buffalo or cow, 'a high-ranking woman', while Kaparia as a form of *masi*, ink. Hindi can also refer to a prostitute as the 'woman of the moment'.

'humbly requests': Jargad interprets the words *bandī araj kahaisī* as 'this slave praises illusion'.

28 *(Bahattarī 57; Granthāvalī 51)*

The commentators interpret this poem as the cry of Equanimity, Samatā, to the conscious soul, Cetan, who is fond of worldly ambitions.

29 *(Bahattarī 58; Granthāvalī 50)*

'cry of sorrow': At this point the *Granthāvalī* has the reading *phoka*, hollow or empty. This word, however, appears in the third line as well. In our text the reading of Kaparia is given and translated. The Gujarati word *poka* refers to a loud cry of sorrow. A different interpretation can relate the word to the Hindi *poṁknā*, 'to have diarrhoea'.

'pipe from a well': The text is problematic. Kaparia interprets the word *avahāḍā* as a form of modern Gujarati *havāḍo*, 'trough of water'. Another interpretation for the phrase *avahāḍānī bok* can be 'the bucket of the well'.

30 *(Bahattarī 59; Granthāvalī 6)*

31 *(Bahattarī 62; Granthāvalī 77)*

'intimate audiences': The word *gosalkhānā* refers to the bath, where Muslim rulers discussed their most secret matters.

32 *(Bahattarī 63; Granthāvalī 29)*

'be mindful': The verb used here, *manānā*, has a wide range of meanings—to cause to agree, to persuade; to console; to conciliate, to placate; to invoke (a deity), to worship, to propitiate; to celebrate; to meditate, reflect on.

'king of gods': Indra in the original.

'the music of farewell': The Hindi has *karo dhanāsī*, 'play Dhanāśrī raga', a raga played at the end of recitals.

33 *(Bahattarī 64; Granthāvalī 8)*

'Where shall I try to search?': The expression *sir paṭaknā*, 'to dash (on) the head', means 'to take great pains', 'to make strenuous search'. In Braj it can also mean 'to be in trouble'. Jargad interprets the word 'wander' as 'visiting places of pilgrimage' and 'to dash the head' as 'to bow the head'.

'I won't make up my eyes like the eyes of the wagtail': Manuscripts d and g have the reading of *añjana dṛga paṁkāhiṁ lagāvuṁ*, 'I put collyrium on my lotus-eyes' or 'and ointment on my eyes'.

34 *(Bahattarī 65; Granthāvalī 33)*

'crocodile': The commentators interpret the word *māṅgar* as *magar*, crocodile, and Jargad extends the meaning into 'fish'.

'Like a crocodile they are fixed on the door of my beloved's beauty': Jargad interprets this line in the following way—'My eyes stare at the door of my beloved in the same way as the fish separated from the water watches the water.' The Bombay edition gives a variant reading of this line: *māṅgara jyoṁ ṭamāke rahī pīya chabī ke dhāra*, which is interpreted as, 'Like a crocodile, it desires to look with a steady gaze at the image of the beloved.' Kaparia notes that the crocodile always has tears in its eyes.

'Don't be dejected, clever woman—the Cloud of Bliss is not far': Kaparia cuts the first two words as *hai jana*. In this way, the meaning becomes: 'The Cloud of Bliss is not far from the distress and prudence of his people.'

35 *(Bahattarī 67; Granthāvalī 65)*

36 *(Bahattarī 68; Granthāvalī 64)*

'how can it be paid back?': *Dīdho* emended from the apparent misprint *ḍīgho* on the basis of manuscripts d and g.

'is used up': The word *ālī* in manuscripts d and g may be an archaic form of the Gujarati perfective *āvelī*, 'came' i.e. 'was used up'. The editions give the simpler reading, *āpī*, 'I gave'.

'the principal': The text is emended here on the basis of manuscripts d and g from *khāṁḍī paraṭhavere mūla āpūṁ*.

Songs Forgotten

37 *(Granthāvalī 116)*

38 *(Granthāvalī 66)*

39 *(Granthāvalī 72)*

40 *(Granthāvalī 79)*

'My dear life': According to Jargad in this poem Good Understanding, Sumati, is talking to Consciousness, Cetan.

'There': That is, at the place of Egotism, Mamatā.

'my dear': Kaparia interprets the word *lāl* as a vocative, while Jargad simply takes it as an adjective to *charī*, 'red staff'.

'holding a staff': According to Jargad, this is the staff of knowledge (*bhedajñāna*). Kaparia breaks the word as *cha-rī* and takes it as a reference to the formal ritual of the six (*cha*) *rī*, congregational pilgrimage, whose categories end in the syllable *-rī* (*bhoṁya-sañcārī, nāri-saṅga-nivārī, ekal-āhārī, pādcārī, āvaśyak doyavārī, sacittaparihārī*). These six temporary vows are taken by all observing lay members of a congregational pilgrimage (*saṅgh yātrā*). See also the references to the six vows in Cort 1990.

'fraud': The word *dumba* is not attested in dictionaries. Jargad seems to derive it from *dambha*, deceit or fraud, while Kaparia from *durbala*, weak, and interprets it as 'light, insignificant'.

41 *(Granthāvalī 83)*

'the gap': Our reading *bheva* is an emendation from the unrhyming *bheda*. Both mean distance or difference.

'dear': The word *ālī* is normally translated as a vocative addressed to a female companion. In its function it can also be similar to an exclamation not addressed to any particular person. In this poem sometimes the lover and sometimes the female companion is addressed. In the second strophe, which clearly addresses the husband, this word is hypermetrical and was probably added to the line by a singer during the period of oral transmission. Another, less likely, possibility is to derive the word from the Perso-Arabic *'ālī-jāh* 'lord', which can also be the address of the husband by a wife in Rajasthan.

'wretched': Here the feminine adjectival form of the Bombay edition is given. The *nigāro* reading of the *Granthāvalī* is either a misprint or a distorted form to rhyme with the following word.

'vulgar': 'Of village birth', used as an abuse.

'the baseless shawl of shame torments me': The text is unclear here. Jargad seems to interpret *pera* as an absolutive of *pernā*, to harass or to tease. Kaparia gives a different reading: *para nirūlī kulaṭī kāna* and interprets it somewhat unclearly as 'another rootless and unchaste woman, Mamatā, blows (i.e. whispers) into the ears (*kān*) of my husband.'

'is knocked down from its roots': The text is unclear. Kaparia reads *jaba jaḍato jaḍabāsa anta*, 'When the end of living together with the senseless comes.'

42 *(Granthāvalī 67)*

'child-murdering hag': Both commentators say that in this poem Sumati is speaking to *mithyātattva*, falseness, although Kaparia in one place claimed that Viveka was addressing Sumati. They say that the boy is 'right faith' or 'right worldview' (*samyakatva* or *uparāma samakita*).

'You're sleeping': The interpretation of the masculine word *sūto* is uncertain. A possible emendation is into feminine *sūtī*, 'you sleep'.

'the five, the twenty-five and the fifty practices': The number five refers to the five *mahāvratas*, 'great vows', non-violence (*ahiṁsā*), truth (*satya*), not stealing (*asteya*), chastity (*brahmacarya*) and renouncing of any possessions beside the necessary utensils (*aparigraha*). The number twenty-five may refer to the five emotions (*bhāvanā*) linked to each vow, while the number fifty to the fifty ascetic practices.

43 *(Granthāvalī* 69*)*

'There are two thieves and two spies in it': The commentators explain the mansion as the body and the two thieves as passion and hatred, the two spies as breath and age.

'five and three women': Jargad interprets these numbers as references to the five sense organs and to the mind, speech and bodily strength.

'A woman subjugated the whole world': Jargad takes it as a reference to the mind.

'There are four men in the mansion': Jargad interprets this as reference to anger, pride, illusion and greed.

'seasons': The meaning of the word *rutlāṁ* is unclear. It may be a misprint or connected to ṛtu, 'season'. If the words are *meru talāṁ*, then the meaning may be 'at the feet of mount Meru', i.e. in the world.

'The Cloud of Bliss understands this song': An alternative interpretation is 'Ānandghan asks for the meaning of this song'.

44 *(Granthāvalī* 81*)*

'bring': The nasalized forms *lyāuṁ* and *gāuṁ* suggest first person singular—'let me bring', 'let me sing'. Since the tone of the poem is that of instruction, the commentators rightly interpret these forms as second person imperatives, 'bring, take' and 'sing'. (Omitting or adding nasalization is a common phenomenon in Hindi manuscript transmission.)

45 *(Granthāvalī* 85*)*

46 *(Granthāvalī* 90*)*

47 *(Granthāvalī* 92*)*

'let lightning strike the barber': The matchmaker barber be 'struck by lightning'. The expression is used as an abuse.

48 *(Granthāvalī* 109*)*

49 *(Granthāvalī* 113*)*

'there's a chance to meet Him!': The setting of the poem is a husband's coming back for the birth of his nephew, upon his sister's return to her paternal home for her delivery.

50 *(Granthāvalī* 114*)*

The text of this poem seems to have been corrupted. It is not present in any available manuscript. The editor of the *Granthāvalī* found it in two forms among the handwritten notes of Umravchand Jargad. Here the text of the first form is given. The second version seems to be more pedestrian and didactic though more comprehensible. In the first strophe, it talks of birth, in the second of a childhood marriage with a husband bought on money and the lack of love between the two. The third talks of the death of the in-laws and of the husband. Then an old woman gives a spinning wheel, which is the spinning wheel of devotion. The guru sat down to card the cotton and she span it in the garret. The guru gave the key of knowledge and opened the door of dharma. This version ends on a note of admonition: Your spinning wheel is many coloured and the roll of cotton is full of *tattva*. One should cut it wisely to cross the (waters of) existence.

'"ay ay ay"': The word *huṁ* in Hindi means 'hmm, yes', but it also reminds the listener of the Gujarati and Braj *hauṁ*, 'I'. A word-play on the onomatopoetic nature of personal nouns also occurs in the famous Sufi qawwali, '*Allah-hoo Allah-hoo*', recorded several times by Nusrat Fateh Ali Khan, among others. One of its recordings is by the Sabri Brothers, on the 1978 Nonesuch LP *Qawwali: Sufi Music from Pakistan* (Nonesuch H-72080). The translation on the cover of the latter gives the following: 'There is the story of the goat who repeated "*main main*" with great pride. His life came to an end at the slaughter house, And his entrails were turned into the strings of the cotton-ginner's bow. When these strings were struck, The only audible sound was "*too too*".' (Personal communication of John Cort). Here the word-play refers to the Hindi and Urdu idiomatic expression *maĩ, maĩ karnā*, 'to be egoistical' as well as to *tū-tū, maĩ-maĩ*, 'wrangling, squabbling'.

'unawares': The word *bāval* means 'mad, crazy' but its meaning may perhaps be stretched to *bālā* child. The meaning 'father' as proposed by Jargad is not attested in dictionaries.

'the girl gives birth to the father': The poem seems to lack a consistent imagery and the meaning here is unclear. One is, however, tempted to think that the groom stands for the Self and the girl for Illusion, māyā, giving birth to the world.

'the husband and wife': The variant reading *bhī*, 'also, even' is better—'even the husband dies'.

'the spinning wheel grants its speech': Or 'the spinning wheel talks to her'.

'The one who wrote "ay ay" on the spinning wheel—look, no one else writes "ay ay"': This line is unclear. The emphatic pronoun *iṇī* can also refer to the spinning wheel—'It is in this spinning wheel that'.

51 *(Granthāvalī 119)*
52

This poem was found by Desai on folio 1v in manuscript 13482 in what he calls the *Puṇyavijayjī Ādi Collection*. See Desai 1998 p. 60.

'the tortoise': A tortoise is supposed to hold the earth.

'the ocean': The word ocean (*sindha*) is an emendation from *siddha*.

53

This poem, so far unpublished, can be found in Rajasthani Research Institute, Chopasni, No. 11634 ff. 23v–24r. It was copied in Samvat 1882 (1825 CE).

'he aims with an arrow': This phrase is slightly unclear. The original reads as *rāsa parāṇā lei sara sāṁdhyā.*

Bibliography

Babb, Lawrence A.: *Absent Lord: Ascetics and Kings in a Jain Ritual Culture*. University of California Press, Berkeley, 1994.

Balbir, Nalini and Osier, Jean-Pierre (tr.): *Le défaite d'Amour of Nāgadeva*. les Éditions du Cerf, Paris, 2004.

Bangha, Imre: *Saneh ko Mārag: Ānandghan kā Jīvanvṛtt*. Vāṇī Prakāśan, New Delhi, 1999.

Bangha, Imre: 'Scribal Transmission and Emerging Hindi Canons in the Eighteenth Century: The Case of the Jain Ānandghan's *Bahattarī*'. *Annali dell'Istituto Orientale di Napoli* 68/1–4 (2008) pp. 19–34.

Bansal, Naresh Chandra: *Caitanya Sampradāy: Siddhānt aur Sāhitya*. Vinod Pustak Mandir, Agra, 1980.

Bryant, Kenneth and Hawley, John Stratton: *Surdas: Poems from the Early Tradition*. Harvard University Press, Cambridge, MA (forthcoming).

Callewaert, Winand M. and Lath, Mukund: *The Hindi Padāvalī of Nāmdev: A Critical Edition of Namdev's Hindi Songs with Translation and Annotation*. Motilal Banarsidass, Delhi, 1989.

Chaudhri, Gulabchandra: *Jain Sāhitya kā Bṛhad Itihās, Bhāg 6: Kāvya Sāhitya*. Pārśvanāth Vidyāśram Śodh Saṅsthān, Varanasi, 1973.

Cort, John E.: 'The Jain Sacred Cosmos: Selections from a Medieval Pilgrimage Text'. In Granoff, Phyllis (ed.): *The Clever Adulteress and*

Other Stories. A Treasury of Jain Literature. Mosaic Press, Oakville, Ontario, 1990, pp. 245–273.

Cort, John E.: 'The Śvetāmbar Mūrtipūjak Jain Mendicant'. *Man* (N.S.) 26 (1991), pp. 549–69.

Cort, John E.: 'Defining Jainism: Reform in the Jain Tradition'. In O'Connell, Joseph T. (ed.): *Jain Doctrine and Practice*. University of Toronto, Centre for South Asian Studies, Toronto, 2000a, pp. 184–85.

Cort, John E.: 'Tantra in Jainism: The Cult of Ghaṇṭākarṇ Mahāvīr, the Great Hero Bell-Ears'. *Bulletine d'Études Indiennes* 15 (2000b), pp. 115–33.

Cort, John E.: 'Worship of Bell-Ears the Great Hero, a Jain Tantric Deity'. In White, David G. *Tantra in Practice*. Princeton University Press, Princeton, [2000] pp. 417–33.

Cort, John E.: *Jains in the World: Religious Values and Ideology in India*. Oxford University Press, New York, 2001.

Cort, John E.: 'Bhakti in the Early Jain Tradition: Understanding Devotional Religion in South Asia'. *History of Religions* 42 (2002a), 59–86.

Cort, John E.: 'A Tale of Two Cities: On the Origins of Digambar Sectarianism in North India'. In Lawrence A. Babb, Varsha Joshi and Michael W. Meister (ed.): *Multiple Histories: Culture and Society in the Study of Rajasthan*. Rawat, Jaipur, 2002b, pp. 39–83.

Cort, John E.: 'Green Jainism? Notes and Queries toward a Possible Jain Environmental Ethic'. In Christopher Key Chapple (ed.): *Jainism and Ecology: Nonviolence in the Web of Life*. Cambridge, MA, 2002c (reprinted Motilal Banarsidass), pp. 63–94.

Cort, John E.: 'God Outside and God Inside: North Indian Digambar Jain Performance of Bhakti'. In Bangha, Imre (ed.): *Bhakti Beyond the Forest: Papers presented at the 10th International Bhakti Conference: Early Modern Literatures in North India held at Sapientia—Hungarian University of Transylvania, Miercurea Ciuc, Romania between 22–24 July 2009*. Manohar, New Delhi 2012.

Deol, Jeevan Singh: 'Sūrdās: Poet and Text in the Sikh Tradition'.

Bulletin of the School of Oriental and African Studies 63/2 (2000) pp. 169–193.

Deol, Jeevan Singh: 'Text and Lineage in Early Sikh History: Issues in the Study of the Adi Granth'. *Bulletin of the School of Oriental and African Studies* 64/1 (2001) pp. 34–58.

Desai, Kumarpal: *Ab Ham Amar Bhaye: Ānandghan: Jīvan aur Kavan*. Jayabhikkhu Sāhitya Ṭrasṭ Prakāśan, Ahmedabad, 1998.

Desai, Kumarpal: *Ānandghan: Ek Adhyayan: 'Ānandghan Bāvīsī'ne Anulakṣīne*. Ādarś Prakāśan, Ahmedabad, 1980.

Desai, Mohanlal Dalichand: 'Adhyātmarasik Paṇḍit Devcandrajī: Jīvanparicay'. In Kantibhai B. Shah (ed.): *Śrī Devcandrajī Mahārāj Kṛt Stavan Covīsī*. Śrī Śrutajñān Prasārak Sabhā, Ahmedabad, 2003, pp. 9–18 (Originally published in *Jain Yug*, 1927).

Doshi, Abhay I.: *Covīsī: Svarūp Ane Sāhitya*. Saurāṣṭrakesarī Prāṇguru Jain Filosofikal enḍ Liṭarari Risarc Senṭar, Bombay, 2006.

Dundas, Paul: *The Jains*. Routledge, London, 1992.

Dundas, Paul: 'The Jain Monk Jinapati Sūri Gets the Better of a Nāth Yogī'. In White, David G.: *Tantra in Practice*. Princeton University Press, Princeton, 2000, pp. 231–238.

Hadi, Nabi: *Dictionary of Indo-Persian Literature*. Indira Gandhi National Centre for the Arts, Abhinav Publications, New Delhi, 1995.

Ivanov, Vladimir: *Concise Descriptive Catalogue of the Persian Manuscripts in the Collection of the Asiatic Society of Bengal*. The Asiatic Society, Calcutta, 1985.

Jain, Hiralal (ed.): *Madanaparājayacarita of Harideva*. Bhāratīya Jñānpīṭh, Benares, 1962.

Jain, Kanchedi Lal: *Adhyātma Pad Pārijāt*. Śrī Gaṇeṣ Varṇī Digambar Jain Sansthān, Varanasi, 1996.

Jain, Premsagar: *Hindī Jain Bhakti-kāvya aur Kavi*. Bhāratīya Jñānpīṭh Prakāśan, Benares, 1964.

Jaini, Padmanabh S.: *The Jaina Path of Purification*. Motilal Banarsidass, New Delhi, 1998 (First edn: 1979).

Jairazbhoy, Nazir Ali: *The Ragas of North India: Their Structure and Evolution*. Faber and Faber, London, 1971.

Jambuvijay, Muni (ed.): *Catalogue of the Manuscripts of Pāṭaṇa Jain Bhaṇḍāra*. Four parts in three volumes. Sharadaben Chimanbhai Educational Research Centre, Ahmedabad, 1991.

Jhaveri, Krishnalal Mohanlal: *Milestones of Gujarati Literature*. The Gujarat Printing Press, Bombay, 1914.

Kaparia, Motichand Girdharlal: *Śrī Ānandghanjīnāṁ Pado*. Vols. I–II. Mahāvīr Jain Vidyālay, Mumbai, 1983 (Vol. I), 1982 (Vol. II) (First edn: 1955–63).

Kharaid, Mahtab Chandra (ed.): *(Jain Yogīndra Śrī Ānandghan Kṛt:) Ānandghan Granthāvalī: Saralārtha Sahit (Saṁgrah Evam Arthakār Umrāvcand Jain Jargaḍ)*. Vijaycandra Jargad, Jaipur, 1974.

Khare, Narayan Moreshvar (ed.): *Āśram Bhajanāvalī*. Navajīvan Prakāśan Mandir, Ahmedabad, 1992 (Twenty-seventh edn).

Kolff, Dirk H.A.: *Naukar, Rajput and Sepoy: The Ethnohistory of the Military Labour Market in Hindustan, 1450–1850*. Cambridge University Press, Cambridge, 1990.

Lalitprabhsagar, Mahopadhyay: *Upādhyāy Devcandra: Jīvan, Sāhitya aur Vicār*. Prākṛt Bhāratī Akādamī, Jaipur and Śrī Jityaśāśrī Fāuṇḍeśan, Calcutta, 1994.

Lath, Mukund: *Half a Tale (The Ardhakathānaka of Banārsīdās): A Study in the Interrelationship between Autobiography and History*. Rajasthan Prakrit Bharati Sansthan, Jaipur, 1981.

Maheshvari, Hiralal: *History of Rajasthani Literature*. Sahitya Akademi, New Delhi, 1980.

Mallison, Françoise: *Au point du jour: les prabhātiyāṁ de Narasiṁha Mahetā*. École Française d'Extrême-Orient, Paris, 1986.

Mann, Gurinder Singh: *The Making of Sikh Scripture*. Oxford University Press, New York, 2001.

McGregor, R.S.: *Hindi Literature from its Beginnings to the Nineteenth Century*. Otto Harrasowitz, Wiesbaden, 1984.

Mishra, Vishvanath Prasad (ed.): *Ghanaānand aur Ānandghan (Granthāvalī)*. Vāṇī Vitān, Benares, 1945.

Mishra, Vishvanath Prasad (ed.): *Ghanaānand (Granthāvalī)*. Vāṇī Vitān, Benares, 1952.

Nahta, Agarchand (ed.): *Rājasthān mé Hindī kī Hastalikhit Granthõ kī Khoj*. Vol. II. Prācīn Śodh Sansthān, Udaypur Vidyāpīṭh, Udaipur, 1947.

Nahta, Agarchand: 'Prāsaṅgik Vaktavya'. In Kharaid (ed.) 1974 pp. 19–43.

Nahta, Agarchand: 'Sant Kabīr aur Sant Kavi Ānandghan.' In Vivekdās (ed.): *Kabīr Sāhab*. Kabīr Vāṇī Prakāśan Kendra, Benares, 1978 pp. 446–449.

Nahta, Bhamvarlal: *Ānandghan Caubīsī: 17 Racnāõ kā Saṁkṣipta Bhāvārtha, Avaśiṣṭa Stavan Mūl. Vivecnākār Muni Sahajānandghan*. Prākṛt Bhāratī Akādamī and Śrīmad Rāmcandra Āśram, Jaipur and Hampi, 1989.

Paniker, K. Ayyappa: *Medieval Indian Literature: An Anthology I-IV*. Sahitya Akademi, New Delhi, 1997–2000.

Peterson, Peter (ed.): *Upamitibhavaprapañcākathā of Siddharṣi*. Asiatic Society, Calcutta, 1899.

Sha, Bhimsingh Manak (ed.). *Prakaraṇ Ratnākar*, Vol. 1. Nirṇay Sāgar Press, Bombay, 1903 (Originally published 1876).

Shah, Nagin G.: 'Ānandghan-yaśovijay-devcandrano tattvavicār (Temno Gujarātī Kṛtione Ādhāre)'. In Kothari, Jayant and Shah, Kantibhai B. (eds.), *Madhyakālīn Gujarātī Jain Sāhitya*. Mahāvīr Jain Vidyālay, Bombay, 1993, pp. 81-88.

Sharma, Siddharāj (ed.): *Vītak*. Śrī Navtanpurī Dhām, Jamnagar, 1965.

Sharma, Devendranāth and Snatak, Vijayendra (ed.): *Hindī Sāhitya kā Bṛhat Itihās*, Vol. 5. Nāgarīpracāriṇī Sabhā, Benares, 1974.

Sen, Kṣitimohan: 'Jain Marmī Ānandghan kā Kāvya'. *Vīṇā*, Nov. 1938 pp. 3–11.

Sudarshanashri, Sādhvī: *Ānandghan kā Rahasyavād*. Pārśvanāth Vidyāśram Śodh Sansthān, Benares, 1984.

Shukla, Devendranath: *Rāg Jijñāsā*. Benares: Viśvavidyālay Prakāśan, 2001.

Shukla, Harish: *Gurjar Jain Kaviyõ kī Hindī Sāhitya ko Den*. Javāhar Pustakālay, Mathura, 1976.

Buddhisagar: *Ānandghanjī Pad Saṅgrah*. Adhyātma Jñān Prasārak Maṇḍal, Mumbai, 1953 (First edn: 1913).
Vajpeyi, Nandadulāre (ed.): *Sūrsāgar*. Nāgarīpracāriṇī Sabhā, Benares, 1952 (Second edn).
Vasant (ed.): *Rāg-koś*. Saṅgīt Kāryālay, Hathras, 1970 (Second edn).
Vinaysagar, Mahopadhyay: *Khartar Gaccha kā Bṛhad Itihās*. Jaipur: Prākṛt Bhāratī Akādamī, Jaipur 2004.
Vinayvijay, Muni: *Śvetāmbar Jain Granth Mārgdarṣak: Jain Granth Gāiḍ*. Jain Ātmānand Sabhā, Bhavnagar, 1914.

Index of First Lines

Read More

PENGUIN CLASSICS

The Roots of Vedānta

Selections from Śaṅkara's Writing

Selected, edited and introduced by SUDHAKRISHNA RANGASWAMI

This erudite and wide-ranging anthology offers a panoramic view of Vedānta in Śaṅkara's own words, with selections from standard translations of his commentaries on the Upaniṣads, the *Brahma-sūtra* (*Vedānta-sūtra*) and the *Bhagavad-gītā*—texts which together form the scriptural canon of Vedānta—and an independent treatise, the *Upadeśa Sāhasri*, on whose authenticity there is unanimity.

Exhibiting a deep empathy with the living tradition, Sudhakshina has selected passages that explain all the important concepts and teachings, including up-to-date deliberations on Śaṅkara. Her general and sectional introductions illuminate and demystify the esoteric concepts, providing a holistic perspective of Vedānta and making it eminently accessible to the modern reader.

Price: Rs 499

Red Lilies and Frightened Birds
Muttollayiram

Translated from the Tamil by M.L. THANGAPPA
Edited and introduced by A.R. VENKATACHALAPATHY

Red Lilies and Frightened Birds is a collection of poems in praise of the three ancient Tamil royal dynasties—Cheras, Cholas and Pandyas. Translated from the early medieval Tamil classic *Muttollayiram*, these beautifully crafted verses retain a surprisingly contemporary tone—a testament to their enduring appeal over the centuries. While some of them are odes to the splendour of the king's country and city, his prowess in war, and the ruining of the enemy country, others reveal how young women, deeply infatuated with the king, pine and long for him.

M.L. Thangappa's translation brilliantly brings to life the playful inventiveness and heady imagery of the original verses. This edition also includes an illuminating introduction by A.R. Venkatachalapathy which places this classic in its historical and cultural context.

Price: Rs 299

The Poem of the Killing of Meghnād

Meghnādbadh Kābya

MICHAEL MADHUSUDAN DUTT

Translated by WILLIAM RADICE

First published in Bengali in 1861, *The Poem of the Killing of Meghnād* (*Meghnādbadh kābya*) by Michael Madhusudan Dutt is an epic in blank verse that has Indrajit (Meghnād), Rāvan's warrior son who is slain by Lakshman in the Ramayana, as its protagonist. But the manner in which Meghnad is killed by Lakshman—in a temple, where he has come to carry out a puja to Agni and has no means of defending himself—is a departure from the Kshatriya warrior-code. This is the most subversive and original feature of Madhusudan's epic, and a daring way of turning Meghnād into a tragic hero. Something of an Indian equivalent to Milton's *Paradise Lost*, this magnificent work is an expression of Madhusudan's mind, of the Bengal Renaissance, and even of the wider Indian modernity that has emerged from that era. Imbued with irrepressible enthusiasm, youthful exuberance and rebellious flamboyance, Madhusudan's voice was compellingly new and inventive.

This lyrical and vigorous translation by William Radice is accompanied by an extensive introduction, detailed footnotes and a comprehensive survey of Madhusudan's use of Indian and Western sources.

Price: Rs 499

Three Satires from Ancient Kashmir

KSHEMENDRA
Translated from the Sanskrit by A.N.D. Haksar

Corruption in government, hypocrisy in religion, avaricious greed in business: these are some of the targets of Kshemendra's one-thousand-year-old satires. So are superstition and sexual obsession, anomalies in education and a host of other ills of the time. Written by a celebrated name in classical Sanskrit literature, these little known exposés of fourteenth-century society find resonance in the Indian subcontinent even today.

Price: Rs 250

Giver of the Worn Garland
Krishnadevarāya's Āmuktamālyada

Translated with an introduction by SRINIVAS REDDY

The emperor Krishnadevarāya's epic poem *Āmuktamālyada* (*Giver of the Worn Garland*) depicts the life of the medieval Vaisnava poet-saint Āndāl, or Goda Devi as she is also known, and her passionate devotion to Lord Visnu.

Krishnadevarāya's unique poetic imagination brings to life a celestial world filled with wonder, creativity, humour and vibrant natural beauty. The mundane is made divine and the ordinary becomes extraordinary; the routine activities of daily life become expressive metaphors for heavenly actions, while the exalted gods of heaven are re-imagined as living persons. The poet's ability to see divinity in the most commonplace activities is an extension of his powerful belief that god is everywhere, in everything, at all times. *Āmuktamālyada* is one of the best examples of bhakti-kāvya—a genre that imbues the stylized characteristics of Sanskrit ornate poetry with the religious fervor of South India bhakti.

Price: Rs 250

The Appeasement of Radhika

Radhika Santawanam

MUDDUPALANI

Translated from the Telegu by SANDHYA MULCHAND

An erotic narrative poem that explores desire and jealousy, love experienced and love lost, *Radhika Santawanam* is the most recognized work of nineteenth-century poet and courtesan Muddupalani.

It is a candid and unabashed exploration of the sexual awakening of a girl, of passion aroused and the anguish of separation. Celebrated as a literary masterpiece in Muddupalani's lifetime, *Radhika Santawanam* was banned by the British in 1910 when it was published again, a century and a half later, with critics panning its graphic descriptions of lovemaking. And, after another hundred years, this epic is now available in its entirety for the first time in English translation.

Price: Rs 250